Keynote

4

Workbook

Richard Walker

NATIONAL
GEOGRAPHIC
LEARNING | CENGAGE
Learning·

Australia • Brazil • Mexico • Singapore • United Kingdom • United States

Keynote Workbook 4
Richard Walker

Publisher: Andrew Robinson

Executive Editor: Sean Bermingham

Senior Development Editor: Derek Mackrell

Associate Development Editor: Yvonne Tan

Assistant Editor: Don Clyde Bhasy

Director of Global Marketing: Ian Martin

Senior Product Marketing Manager:
    Caitlin Thomas

IP Analyst: Kyle Cooper

IP Project Manager: Carissa Poweleit

Media Researcher: Leila Hishmeh

Senior Director of Production: Michael Burggren

Senior Production Controller: Tan Jin Hock

Manufacturing Planner: Mary Beth Hennebury

Compositor: MPS North America LLC

Cover/Text Design: Brenda Carmichael

Cover Photo: A robot drone hovers above a
    hand: © Yash Mulgaonkar

For product information and technology assistance, contact us at
Cengage Learning Customer & Sales Support, 1-800-354-9706

For permission to use material from this text or product,
submit all requests online at **cengage.com/permissions**
Further permissions questions can be emailed to
permissionrequest@cengage.com

ISBN-13: 978-1-337-10417-3

National Geographic Learning
20 Channel Center Street
Boston, MA 02210
USA

Cengage Learning is a leading provider of customized learning solutions with office locations around the globe, including Singapore, the United Kingdom, Australia, Mexico, Brazil, and Japan. Locate your local office at **international.cengage.com/global**

Visit National Geographic Learning online at **NGL.cengage.com**
Visit our corporate website at **www.cengage.com**

Printed at CLDPC, USA, 11-22

Contents

Scope and Sequence

UNIT		LESSON A	LESSON B
TITLE		VOCABULARY LISTENING	LANGUAGE FOCUS LISTENING FOCUS
1	**Embrace Stress!**	Stress collocations Leading a stress-free life	Stress and work Intonation
2	**Media Influences**	Influences Movies and role models	How the media affects us Elision of /d/ and /t/ with consonants
3	**Development**	Goals and ambitions International development	Economic trends Weak forms of *have* and *been*
4	**Secrets and Lies**	Collocations with *truth* and *lie* Lying in a job interview	Making deductions Weak form of *have* after modal verbs
5	**To the Edge**	Describing challenges and successes Facing challenges	Doing the impossible Pronunciation of *had* as an auxiliary verb
6	**Money Matters**	Money collocations Crowdfunding	Talking about saving habits Unstressed vowels: *schwa*
7	**Medical Frontiers**	The language of discovery Drug discovery and development	Making predictions, expectations, and guesses Assimilation
8	**Life Decisions**	Describing milestones in life Comparing generations	Making plans for the future Reduction of *have* and *will*
9	**Technology and Innovation**	What can robots do? Artificial intelligence	Talking about advantages and disadvantages Unstressed syllables with *r*
10	**Connections**	Collocations with *listen* Mediation	Learning to listen Emphatic stress
11	**Life in the Slow Lane**	Slowing down Living in the present	Multitasking versus monotasking Articles *a*, *an*, *the*
12	**Make Yourself Heard**	Voicing an opinion Standing up for your beliefs	Disasters that could have been prevented Reduction of *have* with *would* and *wouldn't*

LESSON C	LESSON D	LESSON E
VOCABULARY BUILDING	**TED PLAYLIST**	**WRITING**
Collocations with *responsibility*	How dance helps me deal with stress How to stay calm when you know you'll be stressed The surprising science of happiness	A letter giving advice
Collocations with *role*	The shared wonder of film The hidden influence of social networks Your brain on video games	A movie review
Prefix *co-*	Global priorities bigger than climate change Which country does the most good for the world The happy planet index	Comparing wealth distributions
Expressions about telling lies	Our buggy moral code The future of lying Can you really tell if a kid is lying?	Expressing an opinion
Expressions about achieving success	A broken body isn't a broken person To the south pole and back—the hardest 105 days of my life The opportunity of adversity	Making a comparison
Phrasal verbs with *take*	You are the future of philanthropy The generosity experiment The antidote to apathy	Promoting a charity initiative
Nouns: *method, culture, approach, role, values*	A prosthetic eye to treat blindness Synthetic voices, as unique as fingerprints The new bionics that let us run, climb, and dance	A persuasive letter
Prefix *ex-*	A warrior's cry against child marriage A kinder, gentler philosophy of success Being young and making an impact	An advice column
Phrasal verb *carry out* + nouns	A robot that flies like a bird A robot that runs and swims like a salamander These robots come to the rescue after a disaster	Discussing the applications of a technology
Prefix *dis-*	How to speak so that people want to listen Everyone around you has a story the world needs to hear Want to help someone? Shut up and listen!	A survey report
Word group *addiction*	All it takes is 10 mindful minutes The art of stillness Want to be happy? Be grateful	An advertisement
Words associated with whistleblowing	Here's how we take back the Internet My daughter, Malala My battle to expose government corruption	An email

1 Embrace Stress!

1A

VOCABULARY Stress collocations

A Circle the correct words to complete the sentences.

1 In today's world, everybody (**experiences / feels**) stressed at one time or another.

2 People who have high-pressure jobs usually (**cope with / experience**) stress frequently.

3 People are always looking for new ways to (**experience / cope with**) stress.

4 There are various techniques you can learn that help you (**relieve / feel**) stress.

5 Doing a sport or going for a run or walk is a good way to (**reduce / feel**) stress.

6 Most of us have to learn how to (**relieve / handle**) stress—it's a part of life.

B Complete the sentences using your own words.

1 I think stress is _____.

2 I think that a good way to relieve stress is _____.

3 I experience a lot of stress when _____.

LISTENING Leading a stress-free life

A ▶ **1.1** Listen. Circle the most appropriate ending to the conversation.

a … you should definitely try it. It doesn't take much time and it's easy to do.

b … you should definitely try to eat more and avoid fast food.

c … you could try talking to your manager to reduce your workload.

B ▶ **1.1** Listen again. Circle the correct words to complete the information in the table.

Advice	Recommendations / Benefits
Exercise	Get out and ¹(**go to the gym / do some exercise**).
Get enough sleep	Try to get at least eight hours of sleep. Do not ²(**use gadgets / watch TV**) one hour before sleeping.
Meditate	This helps you ³(**relax / sleep**) and reduce stress.

COMMUNICATION Talking about stress

Circle the best response.

1 How often do you feel stressed?

    a My second year in college was the most stressful.

    b I feel stressed whenever I have tough deadlines.

2 What makes you feel stressed?

    a I usually go for a swim. It helps me relax.

    b Having to work overtime every day for weeks makes me feel stressed.

3 How do you feel when you are stressed?

    a I guess I get tense, irritable, and tired.

    b I think she's exhausted and worried.

4 What do you usually do to cope with stress?

    a I've been feeling very stressed lately.

    b I've been practicing meditation for a few months now.

LANGUAGE FOCUS Stress and work

A Circle the correct words.

1 I can't imagine (**to have** / **having**) a really stressful job.

2 Have you considered (**becoming** / **to become**) a sports instructor?

3 My boss has asked me (**to work** / **working**) late every evening next week.

4 I'm allowed (**to work** / **working**) flexible hours.

5 My advisor encouraged me (**looking** / **to look**) for jobs with low stress.

B Choose the best response.

1 What kind of job do you hope to have?

    a I hate working long hours. I like to relax in the evenings.

    b Something exciting would be great. I can handle stress.

2 Would you prefer to have a job with low stress?

    a I can't really imagine having a dull, easy job.

    b I definitely enjoy interacting with people.

3 Do you plan to work overseas?

    a I'd love to work in a foreign country.

    b I haven't considered working in the hospitality industry.

4 Do you expect to get the promotion?

    a My parents always encourage me to work hard and get a good job.

    b I hope so. I've been working really hard lately.

C ▶ 1.2 Listen to the conversation between a student and career counselor. Circle **Y** for yes or **N** for no.

1	Will a high-stress job suit the student?	Y	N
2	Would the student enjoy a desk job?	Y	N
3	Would the student enjoy meeting new people?	Y	N
4	Does the student think healthcare jobs are boring?	Y	N
5	Would the student like to join the military?	Y	N
6	Is the student afraid of dangerous situations?	Y	N

LISTENING FOCUS Intonation

A ▶ 1.3 Notice the intonation—the way the speaker's voice rises or falls. Rising intonation indicates that the speaker has more information to add to their statement. Listen and repeat what you hear.

She expects to work overseas after she finishes college.

I really enjoy working with other people.

I can't imagine being in the Army, but maybe in the Air Force.

I'm coping with the stress quite well at the moment. But I'm not sure how long I can keep it up.

B ▶ 1.4 Read the statements. Draw arrows to indicate the intonation you think the speaker users. Then listen and check your answers.

1 Hajime doesn't plan to do a Master's. He wants to do a Ph.D.

2 My parents always encouraged me to become a doctor.

3 My sister can't imagine having a desk job.

4 I considered doing a degree in Spanish, but I chose English in the end.

C ▶ 1.5 Listen. Circle the best response.

1 a So you are thinking of going abroad sometime then?

  b Me neither. I'm going to stay in this country.

2 a So you prefer working with other people as part of a team?

  b So I guess you'd like a job where you can work at your own pace?

3 a That's too bad. You were hoping to get that job.

  b I think you should still consider doing it.

4 a That's a good idea. I'm sure you'll have a great time.

  b I think starting a career is an excellent idea. You're the right age.

1C

READING

Read the passage and answer the questions.

1   Jobs and stress go naturally together—all jobs have at least some stress. So what makes a job more or less stressful? Deadlines, dealing with people, responsibilities, and physical safety are just some of the factors. CareerCast— a website for job seekers— assessed the ten most stressful occupations of the current generation. Let's have a look at them.

2   Coming in as the tenth most stressful job is being a taxi driver. The stress comes from dealing with all kinds of people as well as long hours and rush-hour traffic. Next are field reporters, who have to deal with tight deadlines and may face physical danger at times. Similarly, TV presenters face many deadlines, and, of course, broadcasters do much of their work live, in front of millions of viewers.

The tough nature of the military makes it the most stressful occupation.

3   Senior executives have the seventh most stressful type of occupation. Bosses in all industries have to cope with a lot of stress, mainly because of the heavy responsibilities they have as decision-makers. Imagine the constant anxiety that comes from knowing that a wrong decision could bankrupt the company and lead to hundreds, if not thousands of people losing their jobs. Then there are public relations directors, who have to face the public regularly to explain and sort out problems that arise out of circumstances that cannot be predicted. The fifth most stressful job is one that often involves dealing with problems quickly and requires a lot of organizational and people skills: event coordinators.

4   The most stressful occupations are those that involve public safety and physical danger. At number four, the job of a police officer means being in the public eye and at times facing real danger. Airline pilots also carry a heavy responsibility to ensure the safety of their passengers, and they also have to be ready to deal with delays and technical problems. Number two on the list is firefighting. The physical dangers and demands are obvious, and firefighters also have to deal with the public. So what is the number-one most stressful occupation? Being in the military. The tough nature of the job, both physically and mentally, puts it right at the top of the list.

5   Which of these jobs would you choose, if any?

A Circle the best answer. What is the passage about?

    a What makes some jobs more stressful than others

    b The link between salary and level of stress in a job

    c Top ten jobs most job seekers apply for

B Complete the chart using information from the passage.

Rank (most stressful = 1)	Job	Causes of stress
1		
2		
3		responsible for the safety of passengers; deal with technical problems and delays
4	police officer	
5		
6		
7		
8	TV presenter	
9		tight deadlines; possible physical danger at times
10		

LISTENING

A ▶ **1.6** Listen. What is the talk about?

a jobs that have high levels of stress

b suggestions for jobs with low stress

c qualifications needed for a low-stress job

B ▶ **1.6** Listen again. Circle the best answers.

1 According to the speaker, low-stress jobs ___ .

   a have fixed schedules   **b** don't pay well   **c** have relaxed deadlines

2 If you want to become a librarian, you need to ___ .

   a enjoy working from home   **b** have good organizational skills   **c** be highly educated

3 According to the speaker, which of these is a low-stress job with a high salary?

   a jeweler   **b** professor   **c** hairstylist

C **CRITICAL THINKING** Think about your dream job. Based on what you've read and heard, do you think it's a high-stress or low-stress job? Give reasons for your answer.

_____

Reason: _____

VOCABULARY BUILDING

A Complete the sentences using the words in the box.

anxiety	generation	recession	responsibilities

1 The lack of job security causes some employees a lot of stress and _____ .

2 Employees with greater _____ are usually awarded higher salaries.

3 A country can quickly go into _____ if its leaders make the wrong economic decisions.

4 The _____ of workers born after 1990 take technology completely for granted.

B Complete the sentences using the phrases in the box.

delegate responsibility	sense of responsibility	social responsibility	take responsibility

1 _____ requires organizations as well as individuals to behave in a way that benefits society.

2 In any job, we should _____ for our own actions.

3 Employees who have a strong _____ are usually regarded very positively.

4 Part of being a good leader is knowing when to _____ .

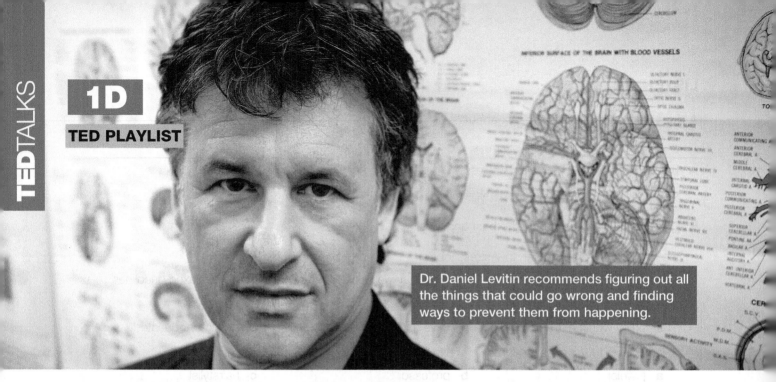

Dr. Daniel Levitin recommends figuring out all the things that could go wrong and finding ways to prevent them from happening.

HOW DANCE HELPS ME DEAL WITH STRESS

Yami Joshi had just landed a dream job and a placement in graduate school when she got into a complex relationship—with stress. In this talk, Joshi and her team demonstrate a 2,000-year-old classical Indian dance, and show how dance can help cure our modern-day stresses and anxieties.

HOW TO STAY CALM WHEN YOU KNOW YOU'LL BE STRESSED

To handle stressful situations, your brain has evolved to release certain hormones that inhibit rational thinking and trigger a survival mode. You are not at your best when you're stressed. Neuroscientist Daniel Levitin suggests thinking ahead to avoid making mistakes in stressful situations.

THE SURPRISING SCIENCE OF HAPPINESS

In this talk, Harvard psychologist Dan Gilbert challenges the idea that we'll be miserable if we don't get what we want. He explains that our "psychological immune system" lets us feel happy even when things don't go as planned, and that we can create our own happiness.

A What do the three TED Talks have in common?

a They look at the physical and mental effects of stress.

b They provide useful techniques for dealing with difficult situations.

c They explore how the brain can be influenced by events or activities.

B Circle the best answer.

1 "Natural happiness is what we get when we get what we wanted, and synthetic happiness is what we make when we don't get what we wanted." Which speaker most likely said this?

    a Yami Joshi   **b** Daniel Levitin   **c** Dan Gilbert

2 Which speaker suggests a way to reduce our stress levels?

    a Yami Joshi   **b** Daniel Levitin   **c** Dan Gilbert

3 "Unfortunately, one of the things that goes out the window during those times of stress is rational, logical thinking ... So we need to train ourselves to think ahead to these kinds of situations." Which speaker most likely said this?

    a Yami Joshi   **b** Daniel Levitin   **c** Dan Gilbert

C Decide which talk you most want to watch. Watch it online at www.ted.com.

WRITING A letter giving advice

A Read the sample writing passage giving advice to a person on how they might manage stress.

Address the person you are giving advice to.

Dear Silvie,

You're experiencing a lot of stress because of your graduate school applications. You're probably worried about which schools to apply to, what courses to pursue, and how you're going to pay for your tuition fees. I have some suggestions to help you manage your stress.

Explain why they are stressed.

Suggest two or three appropriate things that could help them reduce stress.

Speak to a counselor. He or she may be able to help you choose the best school to apply to. They may even be able to help you apply for a scholarship.

You could also start cooking your own meals. This will help you save some money. In addition to that, you'll also be eating healthier meals. Since you live near a park, I would suggest going for a walk or jog every evening. Being in nature will help you clear your mind and relax.

Explain how these steps will help the person.

I hope my suggestions help you.

Sincerely,

Dr Kathy

B Imagine you're a psychologist. Choose any of the other three people on page 24 of the Student Book. Answer the questions to plan your advice.

1 Who is the person?

2 What is their current situation? Why are they feeling stressed?

3 What steps do you recommend they take? How will these steps help them?

4 Is there anything else that they can do to reduce stress?

C Now write your letter. Then complete the checklist below.

☐ Did you use correct spelling and punctuation?

☐ Did you provide two or three suggestions for reducing the person's stress?

☐ Did you use some new words from this unit?

☐ Did you explain why you chose these activities and what their benefits would be?

2 Media Influences

2A

VOCABULARY Influences

Complete the sentences using the words in the box.

| character | hero | ideals | influence | inspiration | role models |

1 Many people find _____ from the actions of normal people who make a difference.

2 Some people argue that action movie stars who use a lot of violence don't make good _____.

3 A person's true _____ is usually revealed when they are under stress.

4 People who share the same _____ and beliefs usually work well together.

5 Many people believe that courage and honesty are qualities that make a(n) _____.

6 There is a lot of debate about whether violence in movies and video games has a negative _____ on people.

LISTENING Movies and role models

A ▶ 2.1 Listen to two people discussing a movie they have just seen. Circle the best answer.

1 Who do you think the two people are?

   a movie critics   **b** good friends

2 Which speaker liked the movie more?

   a the man   **b** the woman

3 Who prefers realistic characters?

   a the man   **b** the woman

4 Who chose the movie?

   a the man   **b** the woman

B ▶ 2.1 Listen again. Whose opinions are these? Check [✓] Man, Woman, or both.

Statement	Speaker	
	Man	Woman
1 The hero made a good role model.		
2 The special effects were really good.		
3 Movies can have an influence on children's behavior.		
4 Movies with simple plots and lots of action are not as good as more realistic ones.		

COMMUNICATION Talking about movie genres

Circle the best response.

1 What kind of movies do you like most?

    a Science fiction—they're a great way to escape from reality for a while.

    b I think violent movies tend to have negative role models for children.

2 Do characters in movies ever inspire you?

    a I prefer to watch movies with romantic roles. They make me feel good.

    b Ones that seem realistic and are based on real stories sometimes do.

3 How do comedy movies affect you?

    a They make me feel really positive about life.

    b I love watching historical dramas.

4 Do you think movies should try to influence people's behavior?

    a I think movies should only be for entertainment purposes.

    b I don't like watching horror movies.

LANGUAGE FOCUS How the media affects us

A Complete the sentences using *who*, *that*, or *which*.

1 The study, _____ focused on violence in the media, was not conclusive.

2 These are programs _____ young children watch on TV, so they should not have adult themes or violence.

3 The director, _____ is well-known for action movies, denied that his movies promoted violence.

4 This TV series, _____ is a favorite among locals, won an award for best TV drama.

B Combine the two sentences into one using *who*, *that*, or *which*.

1 Some comedies make you laugh a lot. They can help lower your stress.
Comedies _____

2 The girl won the race. She trained very hard.
_____

3 One hundred people took part in the study. Nine in ten said movies were important to them.
Nine in ten people _____
_____

4 The documentary focused on the life of an amazing woman. It had a powerful influence on the viewers.
_____
_____

C Circle the best response.

1 What kind of movie characters do you like?

   a I prefer characters who are believable.

   b I think action movies are usually boring.

2 Have you ever been really moved by a film?

   a Leonardo DiCaprio, who acted in *Titanic*, is my favorite actor.

   b *Steel Magnolias*, which starred Julia Roberts, really affected me.

3 Do you think video games can have an influence on people's behavior?

   a One I played the other day, which involved a lot of shooting, was great.

   b Maybe ones that are really popular among kids can affect them.

4 Would you agree that some stories can inspire people to be more altruistic?

   a I occasionally find inspiration in a well-made movie or TV program.

   b Yes, I think movies that show selfless people can encourage us to be more helpful.

LISTENING FOCUS Elision of /d/ and /t/ with consonants

A ▶ **2.2** Notice how the speakers say the words in **bold**. Which letters don't they pronounce? Listen and repeat what you hear.

I saw a documentary **that featured** a really brave person.

I was **inspired to** volunteer after listening to her interview on TV.

Some studies have shown **that playing** video games improves the brain.

People who often **spend time** watching negative news on TV may become more pessimistic.

B ▶ **2.3** Read the sentences. Underline the letters you think the speaker doesn't pronounce. Then listen and check your answers.

1 I was really inspired by the nature documentary.

2 The first three people to call up the hotline will win free movie tickets.

3 The study found that watching comedies caused people's blood pressure to become lower.

4 The program raised people's awareness of the risks of global warming.

5 I'm impressed by the way some celebrities use their fame to help people.

6 The rules are clear: You must be older than 18 to watch the movie.

C ▶ **2.4** Listen. Circle the best response.

1 a There are several superheroes who are disabled in one way or another.

   b Superheroes who are disabled encourage people to not let their disabilities stop them.

2 a I don't really like pop music.

   b I think pop stars who show empathy and respect can.

3 a Social media can certainly have a powerful positive influence if it's used to highlight injustice.

   b Almost everyone uses social media these days.

4 a I don't like watching old western movies.

   b I think ones that feature real-life heroes and true stories.

READING

Read the passage and answer the questions.

1   In 2010, video game designer Jane McGonigal suffered a severe concussion which left her in near constant pain for months and caused persistent nausea. After going through a low point, when she even questioned whether she wanted to go on living, she decided to create a multiplayer game to help her get better. She knew from her research that games encourage us to be determined, optimistic, creative, and to seek help.

McGonigal signing copies of her first book, *Reality Is Broken*

2   The game was simple: find allies, fight the bad guys (things that triggered pain, like light and crowds), and activate power-ups (do pleasant things like cuddling pets). It worked, and her depression soon went away. When she later wrote about the game online, people who were suffering from issues such as chronic pain, depression, and cancer began to play too and found it helped. She named the game *SuperBetter*.

3   Games, especially video games, are considered by many to be a waste of time and to have a negative influence on children. But recent research indicates that they may have underlying benefits. In fact, studies point to a diverse range of positive effects. For example, they can improve problem-solving skills, motor skills, and accuracy; help develop strategic thinking, reading, and math skills; and strengthen memory and concentration. In addition, many online games involve a lot of collaboration, so we can add teamwork and cooperation to the list.

4   Studies also show a link between video games that encourage players to help and support others—so-called "pro-social" games—and similar supportive behavior in real life. In addition, these games are fun and provide an enjoyable way of keeping in touch with friends. It seems that indulging in video games is not always a bad thing after all.

A What is the passage mainly about?

    a how video games can help people get over illnesses

    b how Jane McGonigal recovered from her concussion

    c how video games can be beneficial to people

B Answer the questions.

    1 Why did McGonigal decide to create a multiplayer game?

    _____

    _____

    2 Why do you think the game helped McGonigal with her depression?

    _____

    _____

    3 According to the passage, what are four positive effects of video games?

    _____

    _____

    4 What are "pro-social" games?

    _____

    _____

LISTENING

A ▶ **2.5** Listen. Circle the best answer.

    1 Which statement best summarizes the talk?

      a Studies show that video games, especially violent ones, are bad for children and make them more aggressive.

      b Violent video games are bad for children and encourage them to be aggressive and violent.

      c It is likely that video games have some negative effects on children, so we should probably limit children's exposure to them.

    2 What is the speaker's attitude towards video games?

      a The speaker thinks video games are bad for children.

      b The speaker thinks video games are good for children.

      c The speaker thinks there are more benefits than disadvantages.

B ▶ **2.5** Listen again. Check [✓] the statements that the speaker would agree with.

    a Video games that reward aggressive behavior could lead children to behave violently in real life. ☐

    b Children shouldn't be exposed to the negative stereotypes portrayed in some video games. ☐

    c Children become better team players when they play video games. ☐

    d Video games have a positive effect on how well children concentrate. ☐

    e Addiction to video games can cause depression. ☐

C **CRITICAL THINKING** Use the information in the reading and the talk to complete the chart. Then decide whether, overall, you think that playing video games is good or bad.

Positive effects of video games	Negative effects of video games

Overall, I think that playing video games is _____

_____

VOCABULARY BUILDING

A Complete the sentences using the words in the box.

| exposure | transfer | underlying | virtual | well-adjusted |

1 Learning how to interact with players in a video game can _____ to real-life learning.

2 Using the latest technology, visitors to the gallery can take a(n) _____ tour of the haunted mansions in the area.

3 Some parents worry that a lot of _____ to violent games negatively affects their children's behavior.

4 Most people believe that kids will grow up _____ if they are given opportunities to balance studying and playing.

5 To effectively address the problem, you have to understand the _____ causes of depression.

B Complete the sentences using the phrases in the box.

| role models | key role | leadership role |

1 Parents are usually a child's earliest _____ .

2 The president's _____ has been challenged by the opposition.

3 If you had played a _____ in the project, you would have been considered for the promotion.

2D
TED PLAYLIST

Movies allow children to discover new places, new thoughts, and new perspectives.

THE SHARED WONDER OF FILM

Movies have the power to create a shared storytelling experience, shape memories, and change the way we see the world. In this talk, British film director Beeban Kidron uses film scenes to illustrate how her educational charity, FILMCLUB, shares great films with kids. Kidron explains how FILMCLUB allows students to choose, watch, discuss, and review movies.

THE HIDDEN INFLUENCE OF SOCIAL NETWORKS

We're all embedded in vast social networks of friends, family, and co-workers. We affect them and they affect us. Social scientist Nicholas Christakis explains how a wide variety of traits—from happiness to obesity—can spread from person to person, and how your location in the network might impact your life in ways you don't even know.

YOUR BRAIN ON VIDEO GAMES

Cognitive researcher Daphne Bavelier studies how humans adapt and learn. How do fast-paced video games affect the brain? Step into the lab with Bavelier to hear surprising news about how video games, even action-packed shooter games, can help us learn, focus, and even multitask more efficiently.

A What is the best title for the playlist?

    a How social media influences your behavior

    b Media platforms that provide better learning opportunities for children

    c How movies, social media, and video games encourage interaction and enhance learning skills

B Match each quote to the correct speaker.

    1 "Are your friends gaining weight? Perhaps you are to blame." ○   ○ **a** Beeban Kidron

    2 "We honor reading. Why not honor watching with the same passion?" ○   ○ **b** Nicholas Christakis

    3 "I'm especially interested in a possibility of making our brains smarter, better and faster." ○   ○ **c** Daphne Bavelier

C Decide which talk you most want to watch. Watch it online at www.ted.com.

2E

WRITING A movie review

A Read the sample writing passage about a movie and whether it passes a test like the Bechdel test.

State the name of the movie you want to analyze.

Explain your reasoning for each question.

I created three questions for my test and applied them to the movie *The Martian*. The first question is, "Does the main role show strength of character?" The answer is yes. In the movie, the main character is abandoned on Mars and has to undergo many tough challenges to survive. He keeps trying and doesn't give up. This shows a great strength of character. The second question is, "Does the story involve people working together to achieve something good?" Again, the answer is yes. Once people back on Earth realize the main character is still alive, they all work to rescue him. I think this shows a very positive value: different people coming together to solve a problem. The final question is "Do the characters treat others with respect?" I think in general they do. The main character's team members risk their lives to try to save him, which shows the amazing power of empathy humans have. So, overall, I think *The Martian* passes my test of promoting positive values.

Provide the first question and answer it.

Provide the second question and answer it.

Provide the third question and answer it.

Give a conclusion.

B Answer the questions to plan your writing passage about a TV show you have seen or know about.

1 What is the TV show you want to choose?

2 Think of a question that can assess whether the show promotes positive values. What is the answer to the question? Give your reasons.

3 Think of two more questions. What are the answers to the questions? Give your reasons.

4 Overall, do you think the show promotes positive values?

C Now write your passage. Then complete the checklist below.

☐ Did you use correct spelling and punctuation?

☐ Did you provide three questions to answer, answer them, and give your reasons?

☐ Did you use some new words from this unit?

☐ Did you conclude by stating whether the TV show promotes positive values or not?

3 Development

3A

VOCABULARY Goals and ambitions

Complete the sentences using the words in the box.

accomplish	altruistic	ambitious	aspirations
priorities	struggle	trend	

1 If only he could get his _____ right, he'd do so much better in school.

2 In any society, there are people who _____ to cope with the demands of daily life.

3 With a positive attitude, it is possible for people who start out with very little to go on to _____ great things.

4 Some parents have very _____ goals for their children.

5 In most countries nowadays, there is a(n) _____ towards smaller families.

6 He has _____ to become a doctor someday.

7 Some _____ people spend their lives trying to improve the lives of underprivileged children.

LISTENING International development

A ▶ **3.1** Listen to a talk on the goals and aspirations of college students. Circle the best answer.

1 What percentage of students want to get to the top in their careers?

    a 11%   **b** 31%   **c** 61%

2 Which of these statements is **not** true?

    a Most students want to find a good job.

    b College students are very ambitious.

    c Finding a partner is an important goal for most students.

B ▶ **3.1** Listen again. Match the percentage of students to the following goals.

1	find a good job	○	○ **a**	7%
2	continue their studies	○	○ **b**	31%
3	start their own business	○	○ **c**	40%
4	help other people	○	○ **d**	80%
5	find a partner	○	○ **e**	95%

COMMUNICATION Talking about volunteer work

A Complete the conversation. Number the sentences (1–8) in the correct order.

    a _____ Of course. What do you need to know?

    b _____ Hmm … I guess the first question I'd like to ask is, do you think volunteering is a good idea?

    c _____ That's interesting. Is it hard being a volunteer?

    d _____ That makes sense … My final question is, would you recommend that volunteering be made compulsory in schools?

    e _____ Well, it depends on where you decide to volunteer. Some volunteer work requires hard physical work, or you might just need to talk to people and be there for them.

    f _____ Absolutely! It allows you to learn about a cause, and it's a great way to give back to society.

    g __1__ Hi, do you have a minute? I'm writing a paper on volunteering. Since you've done it before, I was wondering if you could help me out.

    h _____ Yes! I think it should be compulsory. It will definitely benefit students.

B What advice would you give these people?

    1 I've been thinking about helping out in an orphanage this summer.

    _____

    2 I want to do something for the homeless in my neighborhood.

    _____

3B

LANGUAGE FOCUS Economic trends

A Circle the correct words.

    1 The country's population (**has been increasing / is increasing**) steadily over the last few years.

    2 Since 2012, the birthrate in Cuba (**decreased / has been decreasing**).

    3 In the late 90s, several tech firms (**grew / have grown**) at unprecedented rates, but that bubble burst in the early 2000s.

    4 A magazine article reported that in 2015, the economy of Papua New Guinea (**expanded / has expanded**) by almost 20%

B Complete the information using the correct form of the words in parentheses.

In the past few decades, emerging economies have been ¹_____ (**develop**) fast, and many people's incomes have been ²_____ (**increase**) rapidly. As the standard of living has ³_____ (**rise**), people's goals have also ⁴_____ (**change**). Their main priorities have ⁵_____ (**move**) from having enough food and money to cover everyday needs, to having a better quality of life. They have ⁶_____ (**raise**) their expectations and now seek better-paying jobs with more benefits.

C ▶ **3.2** Complete the conversation using the correct form of the words in parentheses. Then listen and check your answers.

A: How has your day been? Have you ¹_____ (**finish**) all ten homework questions?

B: I've done seven so far. The eighth is hard. I've ²_____ (**work**) on it for an hour already and I still haven't finished. How about you?

A: Well, I've ³_____ (**write**) an essay for my English class since 8 o'clock. I've ⁴_____ (**write**) the introduction and main part. I'm just about to start the conclusion.

B: Do you think you'll finish tonight?

A: Hmm … I've been working pretty fast, so I think so. How about you?

B: I certainly hope so. I've ⁵_____ (**make**) plans to go out later.

LISTENING FOCUS Weak forms of *have* and *been*

A ▶ **3.3** Notice how the speakers say the words in **bold**. Listen and repeat what you hear.

Most emerging economies **have been** doing well for the past few years.

How long **has** the population **been** shrinking?

Their charity **has been** helping the poor in the neighborhood since 2005.

Where **have** the non-profit organizations **been** doing most of their work?

With the trend for healthy food, people **haven't been** spending as much on fast food.

B ▶ **3.4** Listen. Complete the sentences with the words you hear.

1 Disruptive tech _____ in many different areas.

2 The statistics show that there _____ in poverty.

3 A lower birthrate _____ to be the key to greater prosperity.

4 For the last few years, people all over the world _____ smartphones to access the Internet.

5 _____ his webinar on creative marketing strategies?

6 _____ a breakthrough in her research? I saw her celebrating with her friends!

C ▶ **3.5** Listen to the questions. Circle the best response.

1 a A Ph.D. can help you get a better job.

  b More than a year, but I've decided against it.

2 a I think they've been pretty flat these past few years.

  b I think the incomes of people here are quite high.

3 a IT is a really popular course these days.

  b It's in demand and the salaries are good.

4 a A lot of money is spent on cell phones and gadgets nowadays.

  b It's good to set aside some money for emergencies each month.

READING

Read the passage and answer the questions.

1   Progress is something we all aspire to. But how do we measure it? We usually think of a country's progress in economic terms: its gross domestic product (GDP) or gross national product (GNP) are measures of how much it produces. These figures are useful as guidelines, but as American politician Robert Kennedy said, they measure "everything except that which makes life worthwhile."

Costa Ricans' high well-being score can be attributed to a culture of forming solid social networks of friends and families.

2   So what does make life worthwhile? Ask yourself what your priorities are in life and the answers will probably be just like everyone else's. Global surveys have found three things that always top the list: happiness, love, and health. Money is important of course, but it comes after these. Statistician Nic Marks argues that we should measure happiness and people's well-being, and therefore created the Happy Planet Index (HPI). This index measures to what extent a country creates happy and healthy citizens; it looks at well-being, life expectancy, and the resources a country uses.

3   HPI data shows some interesting results. As you might expect, developed countries generally score well in terms of well-being and life expectancy, but when you factor in resources, they score badly: they generally use a lot of resources to achieve results. One country, however, seems to be able to create healthy, happy people without using many of the Earth's resources: Costa Rica. So what is Costa Rica doing? First, it uses a lot of renewable energy—only 1 percent of its energy comes from non-renewable sources. And instead of investing in military defense, it invests in programs that help citizens, such as health and education.

4   Furthermore, its citizens tend to have a lot of social connectivity. Surveys have shown that being connected to friends and family is one of the five factors important to happiness and well-being. What are the other four? Being active, taking notice of people and what's around you, continuous learning, and giving generously. It turns out that we are hardwired to be altruistic!

A Which statement best summarizes the main points of the passage?

    a The citizens of Costa Rica all want similar things: happiness, health, and love.

    b According to the HPI, Costa Rica is the happiest nation on the planet because its citizens practice being active, being connected to others, and giving.

    c It is better to measure what is most important to humans, like happiness, rather than how much a country produces.

B Check [✓] all that are true.

1 What three factors are important to the HPI?

    a how much energy a country produces ☐

    b the welfare of citizens is a priority ☐

    c citizens have a long life-expectancy ☐

    d how much renewable energy is used ☐

2 What are the reasons for Costa Rica's high HPI score?

    a The country uses a lot of renewable energy. ☐

    b The country invests in defense. ☐

    c The country invests in health and education. ☐

    d The country uses a lot of natural resources. ☐

    e The country has a high employment rate. ☐

    f Its people are socially connected. ☐

LISTENING

A ▶ **3.6** Listen to a talk about Bhutan. Circle the best answer.

1 What is the talk mainly about?

    a what Bhutan is doing to help protect the environment

    b a way of measuring progress other than GDP

    c how Bhutan uses the GNH to create a nation of happy people

2 Which of these is **not** a criterion in GNH?

    a Traditions and cultures are passed down from generation to generation.

    b The economy grows at a steady rate each year.

    c Environmental resources are used in a sustainable manner.

3 Which statement about Bhutan is true?

    a Its citizens are happy because the government focuses on well-being and sustainability instead of economic growth.

    b Social inequality is very obvious among its citizens; the rich are very rich, and the poor struggle to survive on just a few dollars a day.

    c The country has lost up to 60 percent of its natural forested land to logging and is taking steps to curb this.

B ▶ **3.6** Listen again. Check [✓] the statements that the speaker would agree with.

   a GDP is the best measure of a country's progress. ☐

   b Bhutan's focus on GNH has solved the country's economic problems. ☐

   c The model of measuring a country's progress by its economic growth is not sustainable. ☐

   d There's a growing trend of measuring a country's happiness and well-being rather than economic growth. ☐

   e More countries should follow Bhutan's example. ☐

C **CRITICAL THINKING** What goals do statistician Nic Marks and the leaders of Bhutan probably share? Give a reason to support your answer.

_____

_____

Reason: _____

VOCABULARY BUILDING

A Complete the sentences using the words in the box.

correlation	decline	paradox	surge	threshold

   1 Studies show a clear _____ between poverty and crime.

   2 Research suggests a _____: that wanting to be happy actually makes us unhappy.

   3 Social _____ is one possible indicator of a poor economy.

   4 Some students have a very low _____ of boredom and need constant stimulation to remain engaged and attentive.

   5 There has been a _____ in the number of tourists since the government relaxed its visa requirements.

B The prefix *co* means *with* or *together*. Complete the sentences using the correct form of the words in **bold**.

   coexist: live or exist together, usually peacefully

   coordination: organizing people or things so they work together effectively

   co-founder: a person who starts an organization with someone else

   co-worker: a person who you work with

   1 In order to meet the challenges of global warming, we need global _____ of our efforts.

   2 It's important for any organization's well-being that _____ treat each other with respect.

   3 To live in balance with nature, we need to learn to _____ with other species.

   4 Jerry Greenfield is a _____ of Ben & Jerry's, a famous ice cream company.

3D

TED PLAYLIST

Wind turbines in Ireland. Nations with lower ecological footprints tend to score higher on indexes that measure happiness and well-being.

Statistician Nic Marks asks why we measure a nation's success by its productivity instead of by the happiness and well-being of its people. He recommends tracking national well-being against resource use—arguing that a happy life doesn't have to cost the Earth.

Policy advisor Simon Anholt has created the Good Country Index to measure how much each country contributes to the planet and humanity, and what it takes away. According to this index, a Good Country is one that serves the interest of its own people, but without harming (and preferably by helping) the interests of people in other countries.

Given $50 billion to spend, which would you address first: AIDS or global warming? Political scientist Bjorn Lomborg heads the Copenhagen Consensus Center—a think tank that prioritizes the world's greatest problems based on cost-effective solutions rather than by how serious the problem is.

A Match each title to the correct speaker.

1 Which Country Does the Most Good for the World ○   ○ **a** Bjorn Lomborg

2 The Happy Planet Index ○   ○ **b** Simon Anholt

3 Global Priorities Bigger than Climate Change ○   ○ **c** Nic Marks

B Answer the questions.

1 "... we say that the ultimate outcome of a nation is how successful it is at creating happy and healthy lives for its citizens." Which speaker most likely said this?

_____

2 Why did Simon Anholt create the Good Country Index?

_____

3 How does the Copenhagen Consensus Center work?

_____

C Decide which talk you most want to watch. Watch it online at www.ted.com.

WRITING Comparing wealth distributions

A Read the sample passage about how wealth should be distributed in the world.

State your opinion. — I feel strongly that wealth should be distributed fairly in the world. However, the fact is that there are some very rich countries, — State the actual situation.
quite a few moderately wealthy ones, and many poorer ones. And
once a country is rich, it naturally becomes more powerful, which
makes it easier to become even richer and more powerful.

Explain your ideas. — In my opinion, rich countries should contribute to a global fund.
The fund should be used to help solve problems, such as global
warming and disease. It should also be used to provide money for
poorer countries.

Justify your opinion. — I think we all have a responsibility to help every person around
the world have enough money to live a decent life, with enough
food, reasonable accommodation, and security. I think it's wrong
that millions of people in poorer countries are struggling just to
survive, while people in rich countries focus on having fun.

Provide a conclusion. — It's a fact that a more equal society is healthier and happier. I
hope one day we can coexist as one global, fair society that is both
happy and healthy.

B How do you feel wealth should be distributed in your country? Answer the questions to plan your passage.

1 What is the name of your country? Is wealth distributed equally there?

2 What are some reasons for the way it is distributed?

3 What are some changes you suggest? How could these changes be made?

4 What benefits would the changes provide for your country and its people?

C Now write your passage. Then complete the checklist below.

☐ Did you provide reasons for your ideas?   ☐ Did you provide a concluding statement?

☐ Did you give suggestions for how wealth should be distributed?   ☐ Did you use some new words from this unit?

4 Secrets and Lies

VOCABULARY Collocations with *truth* and *lie*

Complete the sentences using the words in the box.

a total lie	a white lie	an element of truth
stretched the truth	the absolute truth	

1 He said that the project was a complete failure. It's not, but there is _____ to what he said.

2 She insisted that every detail she published was _____. I checked it all carefully and everything was exactly as she reported.

3 She said she really enjoyed my cooking, but I could tell she didn't like it. I don't mind her telling me _____. She was just trying to be nice.

4 He told everyone he had written a book, but he definitely _____. He only wrote a couple of chapters by himself.

5 She said she had never met him before, but that was _____. I saw them having dinner together the week before!

LISTENING Lying in a job interview

A ▶ **4.1** Listen to the conversation. Why did the woman lie?

a The job required Asian language skills.

b She wanted to go to Korea on business.

c She was told she needed to speak fluent Japanese.

B ▶ **4.1** Listen again. Number the events (**1–6**) in the order they happened.

a _____ She started using English for the presentation.

b _____ Her boss was really angry.

c _____ Her boss told her she had to present in Korean.

d _____ They met the client at their office.

e _____ She went to Korea on a business trip.

f _____ She got a job offer.

COMMUNICATION Talking about stretching the truth

Circle the best response.

1 You were sick yesterday, right? Are you feeling better?

    a Actually, I told the boss I was sick, but I was just really tired.

    b Is that right? I hope you're feeling better now.

2 Really? I don't think you should lie like that. What if she found out?

    a I wasn't really lying. I was just stretching the truth a bit.

    b She might find out. That's why I think it's wrong to lie.

3 I don't think so. It's still lying.

    a I think it's fine to stretch the truth occasionally. We all do it.

    b Dishonesty never benefits anyone.

4 I think white lies are fine. But otherwise we should stick to the truth.

    a Really? Does he often tell white lies?

    b Okay, point taken. Honesty is the best policy.

LANGUAGE FOCUS Making deductions

A Circle the correct words.

1 They've never been to Paris, so they (**might not** / **can't**) have taken a picture at the Eiffel Tower.

2 They have a lot of mutual friends, so they (**might** / **may not**) know each other.

3 She's musically talented, so that (**can't** / **could**) be her playing on that music clip.

4 Everyone alters their photos, so her profile photo (**can't** / **may not**) look like her in real life.

B Read the information about Miya. Then complete the sentences using the words in the box.

Miya speaks fluent Spanish. She has 430 Facebook friends and a lot of Twitter followers. She worked at a small advertising company before but decided to leave after a few weeks. She now works as a sales executive for a large organization. She finds the work too easy and is now looking for another more challenging job. She's considering working overseas.

can't	couldn't	may	might	must

1 Miya _____ have lived in Spain.

2 Miya _____ enjoy using social media.

3 Miya _____ have enjoyed her job at the small company.

4 Miya _____ want to work in a Spanish-speaking country.

5 Miya _____ imagine working for a small company again.

C Look at the photo. Write five sentences about it using the words in the box.

can't	could	may	might	must

1 _____

2 _____

3 _____

4 _____

5 _____

LISTENING FOCUS Weak form of *have* after modal verbs

A ▶ **4.2** Notice how the speakers say the words in **bold**. Listen and repeat what you hear.

She **must have** been happy about that.   You **might have** eaten too much.

That **could have** been her at the door.   He **can't have** known about it.

B ▶ **4.3** Listen to the statements. Circle the words you hear.

1 I think you (**must be / must have been**) mistaken.

2 She (**might become / might have become**) the president.

3 He (**could come / could have come**) to the party alone.

4 They (**can't have / can't have had**) many friends at school.

C ▶ **4.4** Listen to the statements. Circle the best response.

1 a Really? I didn't see any missed calls.
  b OK. Anytime is fine.

2 a Yeah, I hope so too.
  b Yeah, he was really talented.

3 a Hmm. I don't think they will.
  b Hmm. I'm not sure they did.

4 a I'm pretty sure it is.
  b I think it was.

READING

Read the passage and answer the questions.

1   If you ask someone if they think lying is a bad thing, chances are they will say yes. In all cultures, we are raised to think that lying is wrong and that good people tell the truth. But dig a little deeper and it soon becomes clear that lying is something we all do—and often for good reasons.

2   White lies—like when you tell a friend a bland and unappetizing dish they have made is delicious—are used to preserve good social relations. In fact, they are so common that we are hardly even aware of them most of the time—it's part of being a social species.

The movie *Liar Liar* brings to light the many instances in our daily lives where we lie without second thought.

3   But what would a world look like in which no one lied? Would it function better? The 1997 movie *Liar Liar* shows us a glimpse of this. In the movie, Jim Carrey plays a compulsive liar and rising star in the legal profession. But following a wish made by his young son, he finds himself unable to lie for 24 hours. Things rapidly get out of hand when he starts having to tell the truth to colleagues and acquaintances. His secretary quits when he tells her the real reason for not giving her a pay rise, and he angers many other colleagues with painful truths. The most disturbing part of the movie is when he finds himself unable to tell the lies that he often uses to win his cases in court.

4   *Liar Liar* is, of course, just a movie, but it does shine a light on how white lies help smooth and maintain good social relations as we go about our daily lives. It also shows that in social interactions, we don't expect people to be honest when the truth can hurt our feelings. So when we pause to reflect on matters of truth, what we are taught as children is clearly not sufficient to guide us through the complexities of adult life.

A What is the passage mainly about?

    a the difference between a total lie and a white lie

    b how the movie *Liar Liar* illustrates the problems that liars have

    c how we lie in everyday situations to maintain smooth relations

B Circle the best answer.

    1 What is part of being a social species?

        a being unable to lie

        b preserving social relations

        c telling lies to become successful

    2 What does the movie *Liar Liar* show?

        a that white lies are a normal part of adult life

        b that successful adults are usually liars

        c that we need to maintain good relationships with others

    3 Why do you think the author refers to the problems the lawyer has in court as "disturbing"?

        a because lawyers are trained to lie

        b because the lawyer is unable to tell any lies at all

        c because it suggests that lying helps the lawyer win cases

LISTENING

A ▶ 4.5 Listen to the conversation. What are they talking about?

    a the benefits and disadvantages of stretching the truth

    b how to help a person become more thick-skinned

    c how to provide feedback to an employee

B ▶ 4.5 Listen again. Check [✓] all the statements that the man would agree with.

    a Bending the truth a little can do more good than harm. ☐

    b Honesty is important in the workplace. ☐

    c It's acceptable to lie to avoid hurting a person's feelings. ☐

    d It's the manager's duty to help people develop professionally. ☐

    e Give advice that is supportive and deliver it professionally. ☐

    f It's important to choose the right moment to give advice to a person. ☐

C **CRITICAL THINKING** Imagine you are in the woman's position. How would you handle the situation? Give reasons for your answer.

_____

Reasons: _____

VOCABULARY BUILDING

A Circle the correct words to complete the sentences.

1 White lies can sometimes be very helpful—(**honesty** / **deception**) is not always the best policy.

2 Most people would stretch the truth in certain situations, but no one would argue that (**dishonesty** / **honesty**) is ever acceptable.

3 His viewpoint is very clear—lying is wrong and it is always better to be (**honesty** / **truthful**).

4 A lot of people bend the truth when they use a social (**deception** / **network**).

5 His (**deception** / **honesty**) eventually came to light and he was fired from his job.

B Complete the sentences using the correct form of the phrases in **bold**.

tall tale: an exaggerated story

two-faced: insincere and deceitful; saying different things to different people

take someone for a ride: to deceive someone

a pack of lies: a story that a person invents to deceive people

lying through one's teeth: to say things that are not true in a way that seems sincere

1 I shouldn't have trusted him. I was _____.

2 My granddad can't stop telling people about all the things he did when he was young. I don't believe most of his stories. He's full of _____.

3 She said she didn't make any profit, but that's completely untrue. She's _____.

4 What he said about being a great guitar player and playing in concerts all over the world is all

_____.

5 He told me how well I was doing just a couple of days ago and then tried to get me fired. He's really

_____.

American Polygraph Association (APA) examiners are able to detect up to 90% of lies.

4D

TED PLAYLIST

According to Kang Lee, children begin lying as young as 2 years of age—and adults are pretty terrible detectors of children's lies.

OUR BUGGY MORAL CODE

Psychologist Dan Ariely studies the bugs in our moral code: the hidden reasons we think it's sometimes okay to cheat or steal—a little. Through his research and his often unusual experiments, he questions the forces that influence human behavior. His studies help make his point that we are predictably irrational, and can be influenced in ways we can't grasp.

THE FUTURE OF LYING

Psychologist Jeff Hancock studies how people use deception when communicating through cell phones and online platforms. Hancock says that while the impersonality of online interaction can encourage mild lying, the fact that it leaves a record of verifiable facts actually keeps us honest.

CAN YOU REALLY TELL IF A KID IS LYING?

Do you think you can easily detect children's lies? Developmental researcher Kang Lee studies what happens to us when we lie, and how and when children develop the capacity to lie. Lee explains why we should celebrate when kids start to lie and presents new lie-detection technology that can reveal our hidden emotions.

A Match the alternative titles to the speakers.

1 New Tools to Spot When We Lie   ○   ○ **a** Dan Ariely

2 Why We Think Dishonesty Is Acceptable   ○   ○ **b** Jeff Hancock

3 Technology's Influence on Lying   ○   ○ **c** Kang Lee

B Answer the questions.

1 What does Dan Ariely's research suggest about human behavior?

_____

2 How does Jeff Hancock believe technology influences how much we deceive others?

_____

3 How do you think Kang Lee feels about very young children lying?

_____

C Decide which talk you most want to watch. Watch it online at www.ted.com.

WRITING Expressing an opinion

A Read the sample writing passage about whether there is ever a good reason for lying.

State your opinion.
> Many people think there are times when we should not tell the truth, such as when it may hurt someone's feelings. For example, if someone cooked a really bad meal for them, instead of saying it was horrible, they would lie to save the friendship. Personally, I believe that we should never tell lies.

Explain your view.
Give an example.
> Of course, that doesn't mean you have to hurt people's feelings. You can avoid the topic or be indirect, but don't lie. For example, rather than lying about the bad meal, you could thank the host for inviting you over or tell them how much you enjoyed the evening. I believe that if we get used to telling lies, even white lies, it may become a habit and lead to larger, more serious lies over time. So my view is that it's important never to lie.

Make sure you have a conclusion.
> By not telling even white lies, we will stay honest and will never get used to lying. And I'm sure that people will respect us for that.

B Do you think there is ever a good reason to lie? Answer the questions to plan your passage.

1 What is your opinion?

2 Why do you feel that way?

3 What is an example that supports your view?

4 What conclusions can you draw from your opinion?

C Now write your passage. Then complete the checklist below.

☐ Did you use correct spelling and punctuation?

☐ Did you use some new words from this unit?

☐ Did you give your opinion?

☐ Did you explain your view and provide an example to support it?

5 To the Edge

5A

VOCABULARY Describing challenges and successes

Complete the passage using the words in the box.

breaking	endured	set	pushed	reaching

Felix Baumgartner is an Austrian skydiver and BASE jumper. In 2012, he jumped to Earth from a helium balloon in the stratosphere, [1]_____ several world records in the process.

Since early 2010, Baumgartner constantly [2]_____ himself to be able to make the jump successfully. He [3]_____ pain and suffering during his preparations, and his team faced many challenges. But every day, they came closer to [4]_____ their goal.

On October 14, 2012, there he was, looking down at the world below from a height of nearly 40 kilometers. He stepped out of the helium balloon, and five incredible minutes later landed safely on Earth. Baumgartner [5]_____ several new world records that day: for the highest altitude jump and the fastest-ever human flight. He also became the first person to break the sound barrier without the use of a vehicle.

LISTENING Facing challenges

A ▶ **5.1** Listen to a talk about Geoffrey Mutai. Which sentence best summarizes the talk?

a Geoffrey Mutai's difficult childhood drove him to seek fame and fortune as a marathon runner.

b Geoffrey Mutai from Kenya became the fastest marathon runner in the world when he won the Boston Marathon.

c Geoffrey Mutai overcame incredible hardships and challenges on his journey to become one of the fastest marathon runners in the world.

B ▶ **5.1** Listen again. Match Mutai's accomplishments to the year in which he achieved them.

1 set a speed record in the Boston Marathon ○   ○ **a** 2007

2 came second in his first marathon ○   ○ **b** 2008

3 won the Monaco Marathon ○   ○ **c** 2011

COMMUNICATION Talking about an achievement

Circle the best response.

1 I heard you finally passed your driving test. That's great!

   a Yeah. I was really nervous, but I finally got through.

   b I thought it would be quite easy but I keep failing.

2 So now you've reached your goal, what are you going to focus on next?

   a I think it's really important to have goals in life. It gives you focus.

   b I'm not sure yet. There are so many things I'd like to do.

3 You must have worked really hard to get a job offer with that company, right?

   a You're right. You have to work really hard at that company.

   b I've always wanted to work there, so I was pretty motivated.

4 Well done on finishing that half marathon in under two hours. That's impressive!

   a If you could run one in two hours, most people would be impressed.

   b I guess my training paid off. I was really pleased to set a personal record.

LANGUAGE FOCUS Doing the impossible

A Circle the correct words.

1 By the time she entered her first race, she (**was training / had been training**) for seven years.

2 A year before he graduated, he (**had already won / had already been winning**) two Olympic gold medals.

3 Before becoming a famous actor, people (**hadn't shown / weren't showing**) much interest in her.

4 He (**was working / had been working**) for 20 years before he (**had become / became**) CEO.

B Complete the sentences using the correct form of the words in parentheses.

1 She _____ (**already run**) for 30 minutes by the time I _____ (**join**) her in the gym.

2 Before he _____ (**be**) 30, he _____ (**start**) three successful businesses.

3 He _____ (**speak**) for over an hour and _____ (**just begin**) his conclusion when I finally _____ (**arrive**) at his presentation.

4 She _____ (**submit**) her novel to five different publishers before it _____ (**be**) accepted.

C Use the prompts to make and answer questions using the correct verb tenses.

1 A: She / see / a koala / before her visit to Australia?

_____

B: She only / see / them on TV.

_____

2 A: How long / you / wait / when / he call / cancel?

_____

B: I / wait / two whole hours.

_____

3 A: He / win / any races before he / start / training professionally?

_____

B: He / win / one race.

_____

LISTENING FOCUS Pronunciation of *had* as an auxiliary verb

A ▶ 5.2 Notice how the speakers pronounce the words in **bold**. Listen and repeat what you hear.

By midday, I'**d** already finished two reports.

He'**d** been studying filmmaking for several years.

How many records **had** she set by the time she was 22?

Had he been running for long before he won the race?

B ▶ 5.3 Complete the sentences. Write the words you hear.

1 He _____ a lot but he hadn't started writing his report.

2 How many milestones _____ by the time he retired?

3 He _____ a millionaire before he graduated from college.

4 _____ for the Olympics for a long time?

5 By the time he turned 40, he _____ in Greece for 15 years.

C ▶ 5.4 Listen to the questions. Circle the best response.

1 a Yes, I have a direct view of her house from my living room.

  b I think the thief broke in last night.

2 a Oh no, that was an important meeting!

  b I'll let her know.

3 a They got a travel guide to show them around.

  b That's good, at least they knew their way around.

4 a Maybe you should look in the park.

  b Maybe you should have looked in areas around the park.

5C

READING

Read the passage and answer the questions.

1 "Genius is 1 percent inspiration, 99 percent perspiration." So said the American inventor of the light bulb, Thomas Edison. It may be relatively easy to have a good idea, but turning it into success involves a huge amount of hard work, determination, and perseverance. Few people achieve great success in life without facing and overcoming many challenges along the way. Let's take a look at two famous entrepreneurs whose perseverance and determination finally paid off.

2 The media and entertainment company Disney is known and loved all over the world. However, the founder, Walt Disney, suffered many setbacks on the way to fame and success. Before he started his first animation company, he had worked at a newspaper, but was fired because his boss thought he wasn't creative enough. His first animation company went bankrupt because he had taken on too much debt, and for a while Disney could barely pay his rent and feed himself. He managed to set up another company with his brother and another cartoonist, but his troubles continued. He lost a cartoon character he had created—Oswald the Rabbit—to Universal Studios, which also took his employees. However, Disney didn't give up. With the help of his brother and the cartoonist, he created a short cartoon that featured Mickey Mouse. It was an instant success. The path had been set for the full-length animated movies that millions of children around the world have grown to love.

From 1928 (the birth of Mickey Mouse) until 1947, Disney himself did the voice of Mickey.

3 Hershey's, founded by Milton Hershey, is the largest chocolate manufacturer in North America. However, Hershey had to overcome many challenges before he started his business. He dropped out of school in the fourth grade. Later, he spent four years learning about candy making before starting a company in Chicago, and another in New York. Unfortunately, both businesses failed. He then returned to Pennsylvania to start a caramel company, and this finally proved to be the break he needed. Encouraged by this, Hershey decided to venture into chocolate making. In 1894, he sold his caramel company to start the Hershey Company in Derry Township and began to make the chocolate that Americans still love today. His determination and perseverance had helped him overcome failures and led him to sweet success.

Hershey became the first person in the United States to mass-produce milk chocolate.

A What is the main purpose of the passage?

   a to show how to turn an idea into success

   b to explain how Disney and Hershey became famous

   c to illustrate the importance of perseverance

B Answer the questions.

   1 What are three setbacks that Disney faced?

      a _____

      b _____

      c _____

   2 Complete the chart below about Hershey.

Company	Where	Success or Failure?
1		
2		
3		
4		

   3 What do Disney and Hershey have in common?

      a _____

      b _____

      c _____

LISTENING

A ▶ **5.5** Listen. Which sentence best summarizes the talk?

   a Entrepreneurs need a lot of perseverance to succeed.

   b It's important to stay calm and not worry about anything.

   c Your attitude and behavior can help you reach your goals.

B ▶ **5.5** Listen again. Number the pieces of advice (**1–4**) in the order you hear them.

   a _____ Things don't always go as planned, but it's important to stay positive.

   b _____ Enjoy the present and don't worry too much about the future.

   c _____ Mental and physical rest is important.

   d _____ When something goes wrong, it's often a chance to learn something.

C **CRITICAL THINKING** Which statement do you think both the writer and the speaker would most agree with? Why?

   a Becoming a successful entrepreneur nearly always involves a lot of hard work and determination.

   b Very few people go on to create successful organizations: not many have the patience to persevere.

   c You should plan carefully and focus on avoiding setbacks, as they will slow you down and prevent you from reaching your goals.

   Reason: _____

VOCABULARY BUILDING

A Complete the sentences using the correct form of the words in the box.

amazement	endurance	reaction	transform	stunt

1 The crowd was filled with _____ as Paralympic long jumper Markus Rehm leaped into the air.

2 Some movie stars like to perform their own _____ , even when they are quite dangerous.

3 You need to do a lot of _____ training if you want to run a marathon.

4 I was quite surprised by her _____ . I didn't expect her to shout at them like that.

5 The new interior designer _____ the attic into a lovely reading room for the kids.

B Complete the sentences using the phrases in the box.

achieve success	direct experience	key ingredients
research suggests	smooth path	

1 Optimism and determination are two _____ for success.

2 Learning is most effective when it comes from _____ .

3 There are many ways to _____ in business, but all of them require hard work.

4 If you expect a(n) _____ to fame and fortune, you will almost certainly be disappointed.

5 _____ that it's hard to be creative when we are stressed.

German Paralympic long jumper Markus Rehm competes during the Anniversary Games athletics meeting in Stratford, London.

5D
TED PLAYLIST

Daniel Romanhuk leads the field in the men's 800 meter race during the U.S. Paralympic Trials.

A BROKEN BODY ISN'T A BROKEN PERSON

Cross-country skier Janine Shepherd hoped for an Olympic medal—until she was hit by a truck during training. Doctors didn't expect her to recover, and when she did, they warned her that she would never walk again. She did. Shepherd shares a powerful story about the human potential for recovery.

TO THE SOUTH POLE AND BACK—THE HARDEST 105 DAYS OF MY LIFE

In 2013, explorer Ben Saunders attempted his most ambitious trek yet: to complete Captain Scott's failed 1912 polar expedition—a four-month, 2,900 km journey from the edge of Antarctica to the South Pole and back. In this inspiring talk, Saunders tells the story of his record-breaking adventure.

THE OPPORTUNITY OF ADVERSITY

Aimee Mullins had her legs amputated below the knee when she was an infant. She learned to walk and then to run on prosthetics, and went on to set world records at the 1996 Paralympics. A model, actor, and champion sprinter, Mullins shows how adversity opens the door for human potential and is something to be embraced rather than overcome.

A Choose the best title for this playlist.

   a People with Disabilities   **b** Olympic Athletes   **c** Determination and Attitude

B Match the quotes to the speakers.

   1 "There's an important difference and distinction between the objective medical fact of my being an amputee and the subjective societal opinion of whether or not I'm disabled."   ○   ○ **a** Janine Shepherd

   2 "I now know that my real strength never came from my body, and although my physical capabilities have changed dramatically, who I am is unchanged."   ○   ○ **b** Ben Saunders

   3 "If you have the right team around you, the right tools, the right technology, and if you have enough self-belief and enough determination, then anything is possible."   ○   ○ **c** Aimee Mullins

C Decide which talk you most want to watch. Watch it online at www.ted.com.

WRITING Making a comparison

A Read the sample passage that compares Jason Lewis's achievements with those of David Blaine.

Write what they have in common. Try to use some new words from this unit.

Jason Lewis and David Blaine have both done amazing things and set world records. They have both proved they are able to endure real suffering to achieve their goals. They both needed to be incredibly fit. However, while Blaine's world record for holding his breath took 17 minutes, Lewis's achievement took many years.

Contrast their achievements.

Explain what the person you chose did.

Jason Lewis was the first person ever to go around the world using only human power. He and a friend set off from London. They cycled through Europe, and then they paddled in a tiny boat to Florida. Lewis then rollerbladed his way across the United States, paddled across the Pacific to Hawaii, and then on to Australia. Cycling across Australia, he then kayaked up to Singapore. After that, he cycled through the Himalayas to Mumbai, paddled across to Africa, and cycled and paddled north through Europe. He finally arrived back in London, 75,000 kilometers and 13 years later.

Make sure you have a conclusion that explains what we can learn from their achievements.

I think that both Blaine and Lewis show that almost anything is possible with determination and perseverance.

B Go online to find out about someone who has achieved something unusual or challenging. Then compare that person's achievement with David Blaine's. Answer the questions below to plan your passage.

1 Who is the person? What is their achievement?

2 Why did you decide on it? Describe the achievement.

3 How does their achievement compare to David Blaine's? What is similar? What is different?

4 What do their achievements show? What lessons can we learn?

C Now write your passage. Then complete the checklist below.

☐ Did you use correct spelling and punctuation? ☐ Did you explain what the achievement was?

☐ Did you use some new words from this unit? ☐ Did you compare and contrast the achievement with David Blaine's?

6 Money Matters

6A

VOCABULARY Money collocations

A Circle the correct words to complete the sentences.

1 He (**made a contribution / earned a living**) as a teacher, but his true passion was painting.

2 I don't have money to give, but I'm free all day Sunday and happy to (**contribute / make**) my time.

3 Instead of throwing away your old computer, you could (**donate / earn**) it to a local school.

4 He asked me to (**make a donation / earn an income**) to the disaster relief fund.

5 She (**invested / contributed**) to a savings scheme last year and (**earns interest / contributes**) every month.

B Answer the questions using your own words.

1 Have you ever contributed time to a charity?

_____

2 What do you need to invest your energy in over the coming months?

_____

LISTENING Crowdfunding

A ▶ 6.1 Listen. What is the talk about?

a how the Internet has changed crowdfunding

b how the Statue of Liberty was crowdfunded in 1885

c the pros and cons of crowdfunding

B ▶ 6.1 Listen again. Answer the questions.

1 What is crowdfunding?

_____

2 What evidence is given to show that crowdfunding isn't a new concept?

_____

3 How do websites like KickStarter and Kiva work?

_____

_____

4 Why are people choosing to donate this way?

_____

COMMUNICATION Talking about making a contribution

A Circle the best response.

1 Are you interested in investing money in an ethical start-up?

    a I'd rather donate money to a charity.

    b A lot of new companies are trying to do good things.

2 What kind of charity did you donate to?

    a One that helps poor children get a good education.

    b I'd like to contribute some money to helping the environment.

3 You've been supporting a local charity recently, right?

    a Yeah, it feels good to give back to society.

    b I prefer to donate my time rather than my money.

4 How much did you raise from your sponsored night run?

    a It was quite a challenge to organize the night run.

    b I got almost double what I expected.

B Answer the questions using your own words.

1 What kind of charity or organization would you like to support?

_____

2 If you were raising money for the charity, what method would you use?

_____

LANGUAGE FOCUS Talking about saving habits

A Complete the sentences using the correct form of the phrasal verbs in the box.

put aside	do without	figure out	break down
find out	look into	come to	take out

1 I hope he _____ his senses soon, otherwise he's not going to get through college at all!

2 Since we have extra money, we should _____ investing some of it.

3 They still can't _____ what caused the blackout.

4 The bus _____ while she was on her way home, so she had to walk the rest of the way.

5 I've realized that I can _____ a lot of things in my life—most of them aren't necessary.

6 He was very curious about the old house and decided to _____ more about its history.

7 My brother always gets yelled at for not _____ the trash.

8 If you can _____ some money every month, you'll have enough to buy a new tablet by the summer.

B Match the questions and responses.

1 How much are you putting aside for the vacation?   ○

    ○ **a** A new car. Their old one kept breaking down.

2 When you add up all your monthly bills, how much do they come to?   ○

    ○ **b** Costs and revenue were pretty equal. Everything balanced out.

3 What did your parents take out a loan for?   ○

    ○ **c** I think $1,000 should be enough.

4 How were the company finances last month?   ○

    ○ **d** They're more than $500 a month.

C Answer the questions using your own words.

1 What is one thing you couldn't do without?

_____

2 Do you put aside money every month? What are you saving for?

_____

LISTENING FOCUS Unstressed vowels: *schwa*

A ▶ **6.2** Notice how the words in **bold** are unstressed, unless the speaker is emphasizing them. Listen and repeat what you hear.

We need **to** save money so we **can** travel abroad.

I'd rather invest in sustainable energy **than** fossil fuels.

I think we should try **to** do without **a** car **and** rely on public transport.

He said he **can** save some of his salary if he really tries.

You can't spend your money **and** invest it.

B ▶ **6.3** Circle the underlined words that you think the speaker will stress. Then listen and check your answers.

1 They brought up their children <u>to</u> protect the environment.

2 It's better <u>to</u> do without luxuries than run out of money.

3 I really <u>can</u> save money by cooking at home.

4 She's the only qualified accountant, so there are many issues she has <u>to</u> deal with.

5 You can't give all your money to charity <u>and</u> keep it for your children—you have <u>to</u> choose one option.

C ▶ **6.4** Listen to the questions and circle the best response.

1 **a** Not really. I think I've been pretty lucky.

  b There are a lot of things I have to do every day.

2 **a** I certainly worry about losing my job, yes.

  b Yes, but I don't think it would last long.

3 **a** No, because they don't usually come to much.

  b I spend almost all of my salary every month.

READING

Read the passage and answer the questions.

1   Buying groceries is something we all do regularly and usually without too much thought. When we buy chocolate, coffee, tea, or fresh fruit, we'll look at the price and probably check where it comes from—but that's about it.

2   The path from the farm to the shelf is long and involves many people, and the fact is that trade in some very common products is not always fair. Millions of farmers and workers at the beginning of the chain sometimes don't get a fair share of the profits. They may have to endure very tough working conditions, and some of the workers may still be children. Furthermore, production methods may not be sustainable, causing long-term harm to the environment. And unfair trade is not limited to food products; it extends to beauty products, cotton, flowers, and even gold.

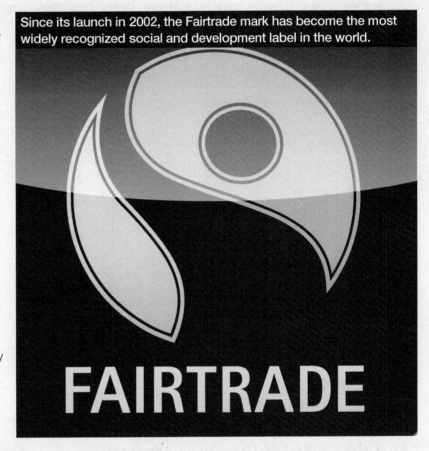

Since its launch in 2002, the Fairtrade mark has become the most widely recognized social and development label in the world.

FAIRTRADE

3   Fortunately, there are several global organizations that are working to provide a fairer system of trade to disadvantaged farmers around the world, helping to empower them to invest in their own futures and to protect the environment. One such organization, which helps workers in over 70 countries, is the Fairtrade Foundation. Products with the Fairtrade label have been produced in a way that is fair to the workers, is sustainable, and meets environmental standards. In addition, a small amount of money from the purchase of every product is invested to fund projects in the local community.

4   An increasing number of large companies, from supermarkets to beauty product providers to clothing retailers, are now working with organizations like Fairtrade. There are now many thousands of different products available, sold in over 125 countries around the world. Choosing one of these products at the supermarket, drug store, or clothing store gives us the chance to make a small but positive difference in the world. The power to help lies in your hands.

A What is the passage mainly about?

    a how products are made and sold

    b how consumers can make ethical choices

    c how large companies are not always treated fairly

B Complete the chart below. Include four issues and four benefits.

Issues with common trading practices	Benefits of Fairtrade
1	1
2	2
3	3
4	4

LISTENING

A ▶ **6.5** Listen to the conversation. What does the man want to do before making a purchase?

    a check an app to find out more about the product

    b post a comment about the product on social media

    c check out all the retail stores that carry the product

B ▶ **6.5** Listen again. Circle the best answer.

1 Which of these is **not** true about the app?

    a It shows the price of the product.

    b It gives recommendations from other buyers.

    c It gives information about the manufacturer.

2 What is each product's rating based on?

    a how many people have bought the product

    b recommendations from users

    c number of comments from users

C **CRITICAL THINKING** Which do you think will have a wider impact on consumers: labels on products (such as the Fairtrade label) or apps (like the one used by the speaker)? Give a reason to support your answer.

_____

Reason: _____

VOCABULARY BUILDING

A Complete the sentences using the correct form of the words in the box.

celebrities	foundation	pledge	poverty	take off

1 The number of people living in _____ has been reduced dramatically in recent decades.

2 The Rory _____ was created to provide support for children who suffer from cancer.

3 The students made a public _____ to donate their allowances to the children's hospital.

4 With the popularity of smartphones, ethical apps have really begun to _____ .

5 You shouldn't underestimate the power of _____ to influence people to contribute money or time to a good cause.

B Read the passage. Then match the phrases in **bold** to their definitions.

Melinda Gates is one of the most powerful women in the world. She co-founded the Bill & Melinda Gates Foundation, and **took on** the main role of running it before being joined by her husband. The foundation **took off** in a big way and is now the largest private foundation in the world. Looking after the foundation naturally **takes up** a large amount of Melinda's time. This work involves **taking in** and analyzing a huge amount of information about global issues and how the foundation can best be used to address health and poverty issues. Bill and Melinda have made an amazing pledge to give away nearly all their wealth to the foundation.

1 take on ○   ○ **a** receive and understand

2 take off ○   ○ **b** become successful

3 take up ○   ○ **c** fill time or space

4 take in ○   ○ **d** accept a challenge

November 22, 2016, President Barack Obama awards the Medal of Freedom to Bill and Melinda Gates at the White House.

Are people too lazy to help others or do they simply not care about the plight of fellow human beings? Why is apathy so prevalent?

YOU ARE THE FUTURE OF PHILANTHROPY

In this talk, author and teacher Katherine Fulton sketches the new future of philanthropy. She talks about how collaboration and innovation allow regular people to use technology to connect and do big things, even when money is scarce. Giving five practical examples of crowd-driven philanthropy, she calls for a new generation of citizen leaders.

THE GENEROSITY EXPERIMENT

Sasha Dichter is a director of a nonprofit organization that provides funds to invest in projects to help poor people. In this talk, he outlines the concept of "impact investing," in which money is put to work to solve social problems. He also shares the results of his month-long "generosity experiment," where he said *yes* to every request for help, and describes how it changed his way of thinking.

THE ANTIDOTE TO APATHY

Local politics—schools, zoning, council elections—affect all of us. So why don't more of us actually get involved? Is it laziness or not really caring? Artist and organizer Dave Meslin, who works to make local issues engaging and fun, says no. In this talk, Meslin identifies seven barriers that keep us from taking part in our communities—even when we truly care—and points to a solution.

A What is each talk about? Match the topics to the correct speakers.

1 how money can be used to help poor people ○ ○ **a** Dave Meslin

2 new methods of helping people ○ ○ **b** Sasha Dichter

3 why people aren't more active in their communities ○ ○ **c** Katherine Fulton

B Circle the best answers.

1 Which speakers talk about charities?

  a Dave Meslin and Sasha Dichter

  b Sasha Dichter and Katherine Fulton

  c Dave Meslin and Katherine Fulton

2 Which speaker feels people can still make a difference without spending a lot of money?

  a Dave Meslin   **b** Sasha Dichter   **c** Katherine Fulton

3 "... people do care, but we live in a world that actively discourages engagement ..." Which speaker most likely said this?

  a Dave Meslin   **b** Sasha Dichter   **c** Katherine Fulton

C Decide which talk you most want to watch. Watch it online at www.ted.com.

6E

WRITING Promoting a charity initiative

A Read the sample passage about a charity effort and why people should donate to it.

Say what you want to do.
> I'd like to raise money to buy cheap solar lamps for people in poor regions who don't have electricity, or who can't afford it.

> In some poorer parts of the world, like Bihar in India, many people don't have electricity, which means they have to use kerosene to light their homes in the evening. Kerosene gives off dangerous gases and there is always the risk of fire. Furthermore, it's expensive. It can cost $200 a year, which is a huge amount of money for these people.

Say why you want to do it.

> Solar lamps are safe and cheap; in fact, the cheapest is only $5. By using solar lamps, people would be healthier, they would save money, and accidents would be reduced. However, not many people know about them.

Make sure you have a conclusion.
> What more worthwhile cause could there be to donate a little money to?

Try to use _____ words from this unit.

B Think of a cause you would like to help. Write about how you'd like to raise money for it and why people should support you. Answer the questions to plan your passage.

1 What is the cause you would like to help? What are its goals?

2 What are the reasons you chose this cause?

3 How would you help?

4 What would the key benefits of your support be?

C Now write your passage. Then complete the checklist below.

☐ Did you use correct spelling and punctuation?

☐ Did you use some new words from this unit?

☐ Did you explain the cause and why you chose it?

☐ Did you describe how you would help it and what benefits your help would provide?

7 Medical Frontiers

7A

VOCABULARY The language of discovery

A Complete the sentences using the words in the box.

> designed   discovered   innovations   invented

1 Wilson Greatbatch was an American engineer who _____ the pacemaker. The device is _____ to help the heart beat at a normal rate.

2 Karl Paul Link _____ warfarin—a blood thinner—in 1930. He was helping a local farmer whose cattle were suffering from internal bleeding. After closely examining the cattle feed, he found that it contained an anticoagulant—a substance that prevents the blood from clotting.

3 Rapid advances in technology have led to many new medical _____.

B Complete the statements using your own ideas.

1 I would love to invent a medical technique that _____.

2 A really useful medical innovation would be _____.

3 I hope medical scientists can discover _____.

LISTENING Drug discovery and development

A ▶ **7.1** Listen to a conversation between two friends. Circle the best answer.

1 What is the talk about?

   a the consequences of humans living much longer lives

   b research that scientists are doing to extend the life span of mice

   c what people can do to live longer and healthier lives

2 How does the man feel about living a long life?

   a enthusiastic   **b** indifferent   **c** upset

B ▶ **7.1** Listen again. Write **M** for man, **W** for woman, or **B** for both.

1 Who is excited about the new research? _____

2 Who believes the drugs to increase lifespan could work on humans too? _____

3 Who thinks that only the rich could afford the treatment at first? _____

4 Who feels it's important to have a healthy life rather than a long life? _____

COMMUNICATION Improving lives

A Complete the conversation. Number the sentences (**1–6**) in the correct order.

a _____ Wow, really? Is there any particular reason?

b _____ Yeah, it is. I'd love to discover a new way of treating people with Alzheimer's. I'm sure it's possible.

c _____ No, I plan to keep studying. I want to focus on dementia research, especially on Alzheimer's.

d _____ Both of them? I'm sorry to hear that. It's certainly a common problem nowadays.

e __1__ What do you want to do after you graduate? Become a general practitioner?

f _____ Well, yes, actually. Both my grandparents have Alzheimer's, so I know first-hand what it's like.

B Answer the questions using your own words.

1 Would you want to work in the medical field? Why?

_____.

2 What are your long-term goals?

_____.

7B

LANGUAGE FOCUS Making predictions, expectations, and guesses

A Circle the correct words.

1 Most people (**will** / **should**) use wearables to monitor their health in the future.

2 With so many medical advances, people (**ought to** / **won't**) be able to live much longer lives soon.

3 In my opinion, robots (**could** / **won't**) take the place of doctors for many years yet.

4 Doctors are certain that this new technology (**may** / **will**) help them treat patients living in remote areas.

5 Mind-controlled prosthetic arms are slowly becoming a reality and (**could** / **won't**) be one of the biggest innovations in healthcare.

B ▶ **7.2** Listen to each statement. Circle the best response.

1 a That would give us time to do so much with our lives.

   b The longest a human can live is about 120 years.

2 a That would be great, but I don't think it will be anytime soon.

   b Yes, some cancers might be treated successfully now, but many are incurable.

3 a Yes, the discovery of antibiotics was a real breakthrough in medicine.

   b Yes, things may get pretty bad if they don't develop new antibiotics soon.

C Answer the questions using your own words.

1 Do you think people will live past age 120 in the future? Why or why not?

_____

2 Do you think there might be a cure for Alzheimer's disease in your lifetime? Why or why not?

_____

3 Do you think robots will take over from nurses and caregivers? Why or why not?

_____

LISTENING FOCUS Assimilation

A ▶ 7.3 Notice how the speakers pronounce the words in **bold**. If a word ends in /t/, /d/, or /n/, and the next word begins with a consonant, the two consonants are sometimes assimilated (joined together in different ways.) Listen and repeat what you hear.

People **might live** to 150 in the future.

Doctors **should be** able to cure most serious diseases within a few decades.

With remote treatment, we **won't need** to visit the hospital or clinic so often.

B ▶ 7.4 Underline the part of the words that you think the speaker assimilates. Then listen and check your answers.

1 Robots might take over from doctors eventually.

2 Surgeons won't be replaced by machines for a long time.

3 New technology has led to many medical innovations.

4 Scientists are developing robots that look like human beings.

5 Medical scientists should be able to learn a lot from the space program.

C ▶ 7.5 Listen to the sentences. Underline the part of the words that are assimilated.

1 That cookie was meant for your brother!

2 The company organized a blood donation drive.

3 My grandfather suffered from Alzheimer's disease.

4 I bought these really cool shoes for a bargain!

5 Mama Rosa's bakery is the best place to buy fresh bread.

6 Scientists have found a way to extend the lifespan of mice.

7 San Francisco's Golden Gate is a popular tourist attraction.

8 The manager called a meeting to discuss the team's next project.

9 Mixed marriages are becoming more common these days.

10 The huge bear charged towards him.

Read the passage and answer the questions.

1 Perhaps the most famous amputee is Captain Hook, a fictional character in the children's classic, *Peter Pan*. Hook's hand was bitten off by a crocodile and then replaced with an iron hook. Fortunately, amputees these days don't have to put up with hooks. Prosthetic limbs have come a long way, and modern prosthetics are now made from plastic, carbon fiber, and metal. Modern technologies, like 3-D printing, mean they can be highly customized for each patient, so they fit comfortably and can be used easily. New designs and advances in technology have also given rise to specialized prosthetics, like the foot blades worn by Paralympic athletes.

Prosthetics now have sensors and processing power to give amputees direct control and a sense of touch.

2 A recent innovation, which has made prosthetics far more useful, is the incorporation of computer chips. These chips can read electrical signals that the muscles send when they contract, and this activates the motors in the prosthetic limb. In this way, the user is able to control the prosthetic—turning, gripping, or stepping—and over time, the software learns and adapts to the user, further improving the prosthetic's function.

3 But what if there are no muscles left after an amputation? A more advanced technique, known as targeted muscle reinnervation (TMR), involves redirecting nerves from the amputated part to a healthy muscle somewhere else in the body (for example, the chest muscle). When the amputee thinks about moving the amputated part of their body, the chest muscle now moves. Sensors placed on the chest detect the signals and activate the prosthetic. The result is that the amputee is able to control the prosthetic just by thinking, similar to the way we control a real limb.

4 As innovations in technology and materials continue, thought-controlled prosthetic limbs are taking rapid steps forward, and are getting ever closer to the real thing.

A What is the passage mainly about?

    a how thought-controlled prosthetics benefit amputees

    b how computer chips are the future of prosthetics

    c how advancements and innovations are paving the way for highly-specialized prosthetics

B Complete the concept map using information from the passage.

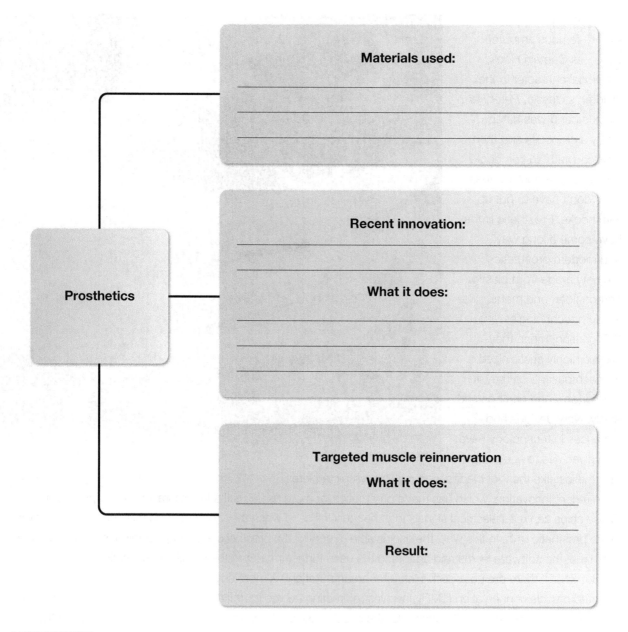

Materials used:

_____

_____

_____

Recent innovation:

_____

_____

What it does:

_____

_____

_____

Prosthetics

Targeted muscle reinnervation

What it does:

_____

_____

Result:

_____

LISTENING

A ▶ **7.6** Listen to a talk about prosthetics. Which sentence best summarizes the talk?

    a Modern prosthetics use wireless devices that are implanted under the skin.

    b Mind-controlled prosthetics allow amputees to perform delicate movements.

    c New prosthetics which give amputees sensory feedback are an improvement in the world of prosthetics.

B ▶ **7.6** Listen again. Circle **T** for true or **F** for false.

1 Modern prosthetics can be customized to the individual. **T** **F**

2 Amputees with prosthetics can't see what they are gripping. **T** **F**

3 Prosthetics with sensory feedback are available now. **T** **F**

4 The speaker says that the future of prosthetic technology involves implants. **T** **F**

C **CRITICAL THINKING** Compare TMR (targeted muscle reinnervation) technique and prosthetics with sensory feedback. How are they similar?

_____

VOCABULARY BUILDING

A Complete the sentences using the words in the box.

customize	modified	three-dimensional	traditional	synthetic

1 Researchers have come up with a slightly _____ version of the original prototype.

2 A hologram is a _____ image produced by a laser beam.

3 During a wedding, the bride and groom will usually _____ the ceremony to reflect their personalities.

4 In many different industries, _____ methods are being replaced by new, modern ones.

5 _____ skin can dramatically improve the lives of burn victims.

B Complete the sentences using the words in the box.

approach	cultures	methods	role	values

1 The company is over 100 years old and has always taken a traditional _____ to advertising.

2 Peer pressure is generally found to increase during adolescence in Western _____ .

3 A person's character is driven by their moral code and _____ .

4 Robots may play an important _____ in hospitals in the future.

5 We need to change the way we do things. Traditional _____ of marketing and promotion are not effective anymore.

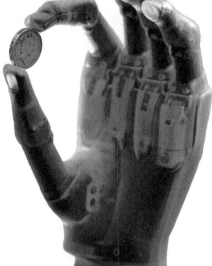

Electronic sensors built into advanced prosthetics allow better aptitude and increased functionality unlike anything seen before.

7D

TED PLAYLIST

Hugh Herr is an American rock climber, engineer, and biophysicist. He's dedicated his life to creating better prosthetics to improve the life of amputees.

A PROSTHETIC EYE TO TREAT BLINDNESS

Neuroscientist Sheila Nirenberg studies neural coding—how the brain takes information from the outside world and encodes it in patterns of electrical activity. In this talk, Nirenberg highlights how this work can help develop new kinds of prosthetic devices, particularly ones for treating blindness.

SYNTHETIC VOICES, AS UNIQUE AS FINGERPRINTS

Many people with severe speech disorders use a computerized device to communicate. In this talk, speech scientist Rupal Patel shares how she engineers unique voices for the voiceless. She believes it gives people who can't speak the ability to communicate in a voice all their own.

THE NEW BIONICS THAT LET US RUN, CLIMB, AND DANCE

Professor and designer Hugh Herr is building the next generation of bionic limbs—robotic prosthetics that are inspired by nature's own designs. In this talk, Herr shows his incredible technology—with the help of dancer Adrianne Haslet-Davis, who lost her left leg in the 2013 Boston Marathon bombing.

A What is the best title for this playlist?

a Using Technology to Grow Human Organs

b Prosthetic Innovations Inspired by Nature

c The Integration of Man and Machine

B Circle the best answer.

1 Which speaker describes how nature can help in technology design?

    a Sheila Nirenberg   **b** Rupal Patel   **c** Hugh Herr

2 Which speaker focuses on nerve signals?

    a Sheila Nirenberg   **b** Rupal Patel   **c** Hugh Herr

3 Which speaker explores giving disabled people an individual identity of their own?

    a Sheila Nirenberg   **b** Rupal Patel   **c** Hugh Herr

C Decide which talk you most want to watch. Watch it online at www.ted.com.

WRITING A persuasive letter

A Read the sample letter to a potential investor about an invention to help disabled people.

Address the person. —— Dear Mr. Smith,

Explain what the invention is for.

I am writing to you about an invention I have made to help people who are blind or who have severe sight disorders. My idea is to create a smartphone app that will describe what is around the person. The app uses the phone's camera and will analyze images. It then uses the phone's audio to describe what it can see. The user will listen on Bluetooth headphones, and they will also be able to ask questions to find out more.

Explain how the invention will work.

Make sure you provide persuasive statements.

The technology is already available, and many people already have smartphones, so all I have to do is develop the app. I hope very much you will consider investing in it. You would be greatly helping to improve disabled people's lives if you do so.

Thank you for your time and consideration. I look forward to hearing from you.

Provide a conclusion for your letter.

Yours sincerely,
Eva Mathews

B What is a common medical issue that affects people in your country? Think of a new technology or invention that could help address the issue. Answer the questions to plan your letter.

1 What is the issue you want to focus on? Who does the issue affect?

2 What is the invention for?

3 How does your invention work?

4 What is your conclusion?

C Now write your letter. Then complete the checklist below.

☐ Did you use correct spelling and punctuation?

☐ Did you use persuasive language?

☐ Did you use some new words from this unit?

☐ Did you explain how the invention will work and why you chose it?

8 Life Decisions

8A

VOCABULARY Describing milestones in life

Complete the sentences using the correct forms of the phrases in the box.

| get a degree | pursue a career | put off | raise a family | settle down |

1 More and more people in their 20s are _____ having kids.

2 In 2016, Minnesota was recognized as the most kid-friendly state in the U.S. to _____ .

3 People wanting to _____ in medicine should consider the stress that comes with the job.

4 The percentage of people these days who go to college and _____ is much higher than 30 years ago.

5 The traditional idea of _____ with a stable job and home is changing due to modern lifestyles.

LISTENING Comparing generations

A ▶ **8.1** Listen. Which sentence best summarizes the talk?

  a Major milestones in life change with each generation and differ from country to country.

  b Getting married and having children are two major milestones in life that have remained the same in most countries.

  c In some countries, an increasing number of people are making the decision not to get married.

B ▶ **8.1** Listen again. Circle the correct words to complete the sentences.

  1 The average age when people get married in Germany is (**20** / **33**).

  2 People are choosing to marry later or not at all because there is less pressure from (**society** / **the opposite sex**).

  3 In 1960, more than (**seven** / **nine**) out of ten people in the United States were married; however, today, less than (**25** / **50**) percent are.

  4 In countries like Japan and Australia, the average age for women to have their first child is (**around 18** / **over 30**). However, more and more women are choosing not to have children.

  5 Marriage is still common. In most countries, (**50** / **80**) percent of people are married by the time they reach the age of (**50** / **80**).

COMMUNICATION Talking about adult responsibilities

A Complete the conversation. Number the sentences (**1–7**) in the correct order.

a _____ Lucky I had this talk with you. Otherwise I might have ended up making the biggest mistake of my life!

b _____ Yeah, that's a wise decision. Buying an apartment is a big responsibility. You need to make sure you can afford it, otherwise, you might end up not being able to repay the bank.

c _1_ Hey, I saw this really nice apartment just a few blocks away from where I work. I'm thinking of buying it.

d _____ Well, they are. But I think I can afford it. I'm expecting a raise at work soon.

e _____ Hmm … aren't prices expensive around that area?

f _____ That's good news … but what if you purchase the apartment and don't get the raise?

g _____ Hmm … I never thought of that actually. I guess you're right. Perhaps I should wait.

B Answer the questions using your own words.

1 When do you think is a good age to start a family?

_____

2 Do you think you'll be ready to make a major purchase (like a house or car) soon?

_____

8B

LANGUAGE FOCUS Making plans for the future

A Circle the correct words.

1 She'll have (**finished** / **been finishing**) university by this time next year.

2 How long will you (**have been studying** / **study**) English by the time you graduate?

3 By next January, he'll (**be living** / **have lived**) in this city for four years.

4 By the time we get married, we'll (**have been dating** / **be dating**) for seven years.

5 By the time my brother turns 20, I'll have (**graduated** / **been graduating**) from college.

B Circle the best response.

1 How long will you have worked here by the time you finish your contract?

    a Let me see … almost seven years!   **b** I guess probably early next year.

2 I'll have been working at this company for ten years next month.

    a Yes, that's right. How time flies!   **b** How long have you worked at the company?

3 By this time next year, she'll have gotten married.

    a She's only 20—I think it's way too young.   **b** When did she get married?

4 Will your father have retired by the end of the year?

    a Yes, he expects to retire in a couple of years.   **b** No, he wants to continue working for a couple more years.

C Complete the sentences using your own words.

1 By this time next year, I'll have _____.

2 _____ by the end of this year.

3 I'll have _____ in five years.

LISTENING FOCUS Reduction of *have* and *will*

A ▶ **8.2** When used as auxiliary verbs, *will* and *have* are usually unstressed and can be difficult to hear. In a negative sentence, *won't* is usually stressed, but *have* remains unstressed. Listen and repeat what you hear.

She'**ll have** moved house by October.

They'**ll have** been living in San Francisco for six months soon.

I **won't have** left town by then.

He **won't have** finished work by that time.

B ▶ **8.3** Complete the sentences. Write the words you hear.

1 _____ university in three years.

2 _____ your driving test by the end of the year.

3 _____ his homework by then.

4 _____ in Hawaii by this time next week.

5 _____ my new job when you next see me.

C ▶ **8.4** Listen to the statements. Circle the best response.

1 a Yeah? Why did he leave?

 b Wow, that's a long time.

2 a OK. I'll call at five.

 b OK. How about seven?

3 a Great. What are your plans after that?

 b So what are you going to do now?

4 a Wow, well done!

 b Have you finished it yet?

READING

Read the passage and answer the questions.

1   At what age are we happiest? Maybe 16? Or a still youthful but more mature 30? Or perhaps 65, when we are retired and relaxed? It's a simple question, but, unsurprisingly, the answer people give depends a lot on their age and situation. As we progress from childhood to adulthood to middle age and then old age, our lives change enormously. We reach important milestones, and we take on different responsibilities; our priorities change accordingly and naturally influence our sense of well-being.

2   Studies indicate that, on average, we become less happy from our early 20s until we reach our early 50s. Why is this so? We may be physically in our prime in our 20s, but many people have a lot of stress at work and are still working out who they are and what their values are. In addition, we are competing with and comparing ourselves to other people as we lay a foundation for our futures and try to establish our careers.

Each stage of life brings about different stages of happiness. But when are we at our happiest?

3   In our 30s, we typically pass several major milestones, such as establishing a career, getting married or finding with a long-term partner, owning a house, and having children. Although we are generally more self-confident in our 30s than in our 20s, work and social responsibilities grow, and with them, so do our levels of stress.

4   Various studies show that we are least happy in our 40s and early 50s, with men less satisfied on average than women. One reason is that at this time, many people are raising children at the same time as looking after elderly parents. Many people at this age also have serious work responsibilities and may begin to worry about retirement.

5   However, the good news is that after this point, people on average become increasingly happy and satisfied. Studies indicate that we are happiest in life in our 60s and 70s. At this age, people typically have come to terms with aging, are no longer competing with others for jobs, and are retired and so have time for leisure activities. Only when we reach our 80s does our sense of well-being begin to drop, but it is still higher than it is for younger people. So whatever age you are now, you can probably look forward to being happier and more satisfied in the future.

A Which statement best summarizes the reading?

  a As we go through life, we pass through a series of important milestones, such as getting married and having children.

  b People's sense of satisfaction with life varies throughout life, and, on average, they are happiest from their 50s right through to old age.

  c Studies show that people tend to be less happy in their 20s and 30s, probably because they are stressed and lack confidence.

B Complete the table using information from the passage.

When we are in our ...	Characteristics
20s	Physically in our [1] _____ but a lot of [2] _____
30s	Reach milestones: owning [3] _____ having [4] _____ Generally more [5] _____ than in our 20s; but with added work and social responsibilities
40s and early 50s	Least [6] _____ period Men [7] _____
60s and 70s	People are [8] _____
80s and beyond	[9] _____ begins to reduce; still [10] _____ than younger people

LISTENING

A ▶ **8.5** Listen to a conversation between two people. Circle the best answers.

  1 Which sentence correctly describes who the speakers are?

    a They are company colleagues.

    b They are college students.

    c They are friends in their 30s.

  2 What is the main topic of the conversation?

    a marriage and children

    b jobs and careers

    c future plans and life milestones

  3 Which speaker is more interested in settling down?

    a the man   **b** the woman   **c** neither of them

B ▶ 8.5 Listen again. Write **M** for man or **W** for woman.

Which speaker . . .

1 found high school hard?　　　　　　　　_____

2 is concerned about the future?　　　　_____

3 wants a career?　　　　　　　　　　　_____

4 doesn't want to settle down?　　　　　_____

5 wants to do volunteer work?　　　　　_____

C **CRITICAL THINKING** Think about your future plans and the milestones you want to reach. Are you more like the man or the woman? Give reasons for your choice.

_____

Reason: _____

VOCABULARY BUILDING

A Complete the sentences using the correct form of the words and phrases in the box.

coast	defining moment	extend	peak	trivialize

1 For most people, happiness _____ after the age of 60.

2 With the age of retirement increasing, people's working lives have been _____ .

3 A lot of young people think it's fine to _____ all through their 20s.

4 Last week's news report _____ the problems that old people face.

5 Surviving a serious accident can become a(n) _____ in a person's life.

B The words below all contain the prefix *ex-*, which has the meaning of *out of, up*, or *without*. Complete the sentences using the correct form of the words in **bold** below.

exceed: to be more than a certain amount

exception: something not included in a rule or group

exchange: to swap something for something else

exclude: to not include something

extinct: no longer living

exploit: to use something to help you, often unfairly

1 There is increasing pressure on companies that sometimes _____ children.

2 It's dangerous to _____ the speed limit.

3 There are always _____ to any rule.

4 Dinosaurs became _____ about 60 million years ago.

5 The police say the evidence does not _____ the possibility that the victim was murdered.

6 He _____ the sweater she had given him for a tie.

Volunteers and students at the Marianne-Cohn-Schule special education support center in Berlin, Germany

Memory Banda's work helps girls to finish school and live safe from violence in Malawi, a country where more than half the girls are married as children. In this talk, Banda explains how she championed a successful national campaign that led to landmark legislation outlawing child marriage in Malawi.

According to Alain de Botton, "The thing about a successful life is, a lot of the time, our ideas of what it would mean to live successfully are not our own. They are sucked in from other people." He urges us to examine our ideas of success and failure—and question the assumptions underlying these ideas.

In this talk, Natalie Warne calls on young people not to let age stop them from changing the world. When just 17, Warne learned about a campaign to rescue Ugandan child soldiers. She describes how she helped get the campaign featured on the Oprah Winfrey show, a victory that helped lead to legislation to help these children.

A Match the talk titles to the correct speakers.

1 A Kinder, Gentler Philosophy of Success ○   ○ **a** Memory Banda

2 Being Young and Making an Impact ○   ○ **b** Alain de Botton

3 A Warrior's Cry Against Child Marriage ○   ○ **c** Natalie Warne

B Circle the best answers.

1 Which speakers helped to create new laws?

  a Memory Banda and Alain de Botton   **b** Alain de Botton and Natalie Warne   **c** Memory Banda and Natalie Warne

2 What is the main message of Warne's talk?

  a We need to protect children from being used as soldiers.   **b** Age should not be a barrier to doing good.   **c** Celebrities can help make a difference.

3 "We should focus on our ideas, and make sure that we own them; that we are truly the authors of our own ambitions." Which speaker most likely said this?

  a Memory Banda   **b** Alain de Botton   **c** Natalie Warne

C Decide which talk you most want to watch. Watch it online at www.ted.com.

8E

WRITING An advice column

A Read the sample letter from an advice column.

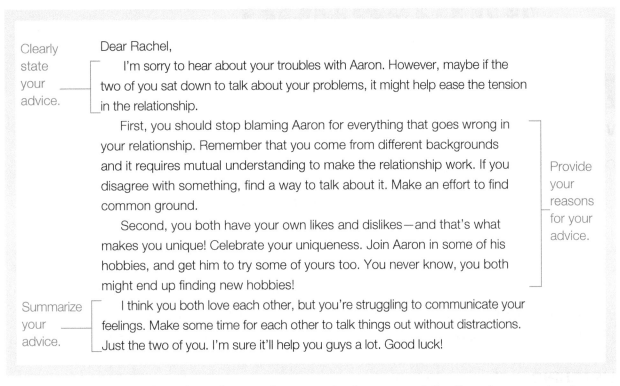

Clearly state your advice.

Dear Rachel,

I'm sorry to hear about your troubles with Aaron. However, maybe if the two of you sat down to talk about your problems, it might help ease the tension in the relationship.

Provide your reasons for your advice.

First, you should stop blaming Aaron for everything that goes wrong in your relationship. Remember that you come from different backgrounds and it requires mutual understanding to make the relationship work. If you disagree with something, find a way to talk about it. Make an effort to find common ground.

Second, you both have your own likes and dislikes—and that's what makes you unique! Celebrate your uniqueness. Join Aaron in some of his hobbies, and get him to try some of yours too. You never know, you both might end up finding new hobbies!

Summarize your advice.

I think you both love each other, but you're struggling to communicate your feelings. Make some time for each other to talk things out without distractions. Just the two of you. I'm sure it'll help you guys a lot. Good luck!

B Imagine you write an advice column for an online magazine for young adults. One of your readers has written in, asking you for advice. Answer the questions to plan your reply.

Guy is a 24-year-old graduate who has just quit his job as a data analyst. He worked for two years at the company but didn't enjoy the job, and is now considering traveling overseas for several months. He's always wanted to travel and never had the chance, but his parents are worried he might lose the chance of pursuing a career if he takes a long break. Should he travel, or look for another job and hope it's more interesting?

1 What options does Guy have?

2 What advice do you want to give Guy?

3 What are your reasons?

C Now write your reply. Then complete the checklist below.

☐ Did you use correct spelling and punctuation?

☐ Did you give clear advice?

☐ Did you use some new words from this unit?

☐ Did you explain your reasons to Guy?

9 Technology and Innovation

9A

VOCABULARY What can robots do?

Complete the sentences using the words in the box.

assembled	function	program	remote-controlled	operate

1 High-tech gadgets are often designed in one country and _____ in another.

2 The main _____ of robots is to assist humans in carrying out labor-intensive jobs.

3 Drones and other _____ devices are likely to change the way we transport goods.

4 Scientists are able to _____ robots on Mars from millions of kilometers away.

5 Nowadays, engineers can _____ a computer to learn by itself.

LISTENING Artificial intelligence

A ▶ 9.1 Listen to a talk about robots. What is the main idea of the talk?

a how to create robots that can help humans

b how robots can help get rid of disease and poverty

c how artificial intelligence could pose a threat to humankind

B ▶ 9.1 Listen again. Complete the summary using information from the talk.

Why are robots a threat?

- humans are limited by [1]_____

- robots have the potential to learn and [2]_____ faster

- robots may eventually be able to assemble themselves and take over the world

What is the solution?

- need to be able to [3]_____ robots

- in order to do this, there must be strong procedures put in place

Why can't we get rid of robots?

- there is a lot of potential for robots to [4]_____

- they can help in times of disasters, and do dangerous jobs

- robots may even be able to help get rid of disease and poverty

COMMUNICATION Talking about technological devices

Circle the best response.

1 What's the best thing about your fitness app?

   a It's great for monitoring my sleep.

   b It would be great if it could monitor my heart rate.

2 My personal robot is amazing. Check it out.

   a Would you like your own robot?

   b Cool. Is it easy to operate?

3 So how do you like your new virtual reality headset?

   a It's really great for action games.

   b Yes, I really like it.

4 What do you use your drone for?

   a Yes, I usually use it a lot.

   b I usually use it to take videos.

LANGUAGE FOCUS Talking about advantages and disadvantages

A Match the two parts of the sentences.

1 If we all had personal robots, ○	○	**a** he asked you out on a date?
2 If you buy that smartwatch, ○	○	**b** you wouldn't waste so much food.
3 There'll be fewer accidents ○	○	**c** we wouldn't have to do any chores.
4 If you bought a smart fridge, ○	○	**d** if everyone uses driverless cars in the future.
5 What would you say if ○	○	**e** you'll be able to monitor your heart rate.

B Complete the sentences using the correct form of the words in parentheses.

1 He's coming to the party tomorrow. If I _____ (**see**) him, I'll give him the message.

2 If I _____ (**be**) a millionaire, I'd still work just to keep myself occupied.

3 Should I buy the new phone now or should I _____ (**wait**) until payday?

4 Where would you go if you _____ (**can**) go anywhere in the world?

5 If there are any more problems with the prototype, I _____ (**cancel**) the program.

6 If I _____ (**be**) you, I'd go ahead and buy that robot.

7 If they _____ (**approve**) my proposal, I'll use my research to help the poor.

C ▶ **9.2** Listen to each question and choose the best response.

1 a I'd use it to track my runs.

   b I'll use it every day for my runs.

2 a I think the roads would be much safer.

   b I'll order a pizza for dinner.

3 a She'd buy a Porsche with the money.

   b She helped the less fortunate with the money.

4 a They were kind enough to offer me the job.

   b No, the terms are terrible!

LISTENING FOCUS Unstressed syllables with *r*

A ▶ **9.3** The vowel in unstressed syllables with *r* is commonly pronounced weakly or not pronounced at all. Listen and repeat what you hear.

What's your **favorite** smartphone app?

I saw a really **interesting** movie about robots.

If AI gained control over humans, life would be **miserable**.

Rapid innovation in technology leads to very **different** lifestyles.

B ▶ **9.4** Cross out the vowels in the words in **bold** that you think are not pronounced or pronounced weakly. Then listen and check your answers.

1 Soon, **everybody** will have a smartphone.

2 My fitness tracker records my **average** heartrate.

3 This app monitors the **temperature** of my living room.

4 He bought a **camera** with his first paycheck.

5 There are **several** good cafés in the neighborhood.

C ▶ **9.5** Listen. Circle the sentence that is closest in meaning to what you hear.

1 a It didn't take long for her to learn how to use the device.

   b She quickly performed surgery on the device.

2 a Robots have been taught to carry out difficult missions.

   b Robots will be able to carry out difficult medical operations.

3 a In the future, military soldiers will become like robots.

   b The army will have more robots in the future.

4 a The professor did not explain what had gone wrong.

   b The professor did not have enough facts on what had gone wrong.

5 a The contaminated batch needs to be kept away from the rest of the products.

   b All the products have been contaminated.

READING

Read the passage and answer the questions.

1 The Industrial Revolution, which began in England in the mid-18th century, caused enormous change and disruption to people's lives. Machines began to do jobs that humans had done until that point. Around 100 years later, there was a second industrial revolution as electricity enabled mass production of goods. A third industrial revolution took place in the later part of the 20th century; this came from the introduction of computers and IT, which resulted in the automation of manufacturing.

2 Today, we are entering a fourth industrial revolution—this time because of recent, very rapid changes in technology, especially in robotics and artificial intelligence. These new technologies hold great promise in curing and preventing diseases, improving agricultural output, and enhancing our general quality of life. However, experts also predict that they will have a disruptive effect on the labor market. Research suggests that nearly half of all the work done in the United States could be done by machines. This represents an amazing $2 trillion in lost wages. And it's even more in manufacturing: nearly 60 percent of jobs could be done by robots.

A production line at the Ford motor plant in 1914.

Researchers in Spain have developed a humanoid robot for automative assembly tasks.

3 *Cobots*, or collaborative robots, are a new type of industrial robot. They are cheaper, and can easily be programmed and moved. This makes them more advanced than the heavy, fixed, and expensive robotic arms that are currently used in factories. Over the coming years, cobots are likely to replace many humans in small and medium-sized companies, which account for 70 percent of global manufacturing.

4 Other industries will also be affected by new technology. In the food services sector, which includes cooks and servers, over seven in ten jobs may be replaced by machines and robots. In the retail industry, half of all jobs could be done by robots. Even office workers will be affected as machines get better at understanding human speech; studies indicate that two in three people working in finance and insurance may lose their jobs.

5 Despite these pessimistic predictions, there is still an opportunity for governments to make sure that the new technology complements—rather than harms—the way we live, work, and relate to one another. Societies around the world successfully made it through the first three industrial revolutions. It is up to us to ensure that the new technology from the fourth industrial revolution is developed responsibly and wisely. Through proper governance, we may be able to avoid mass unemployment and greater inequality, and instead, improve people's lives through better healthcare, education, and connectivity.

A What is the passage mainly about?

    a robots, technology, and artificial intelligence

    b the Industrial Revolution and how it changed people's lives

    c how the next industrial revolution will affect society and jobs

B Answer the questions.

    1 What triggered these industrial revolutions?

        a First industrial revolution: _____

        b Second industrial revolution: _____

        c Third industrial revolution: _____

        d Fourth industrial revolution: _____

    2 What are cobots? What are the benefits of using cobots?

        _____

        _____

    3 What are the disadvantages of introducing cobots?

        _____

        _____

LISTENING

A ▶ **9.6** Listen. Which sentence best summarizes the talk?

    a The fourth industrial revolution will be a time of great change that requires people to adapt and learn new skills.

    b The fourth industrial revolution will impact children the most.

    c The fourth industrial revolution resulted in a lot of people losing their jobs.

B ▶ **9.6** Listen again. Check [✓] the predictions mentioned by the speaker.

    a The changes will be smaller than in previous revolutions. ☐

    b 65 percent of children entering primary school now will end up jobless. ☐

    c People will work together with robots. ☐

    d Humanity will adapt to this revolution and carry on. ☐

    e Robots will adapt and take over the workforce. ☐

C CRITICAL THINKING Check [✓] the statements that both the author and speaker are most likely to agree with.

a There will be minimal job losses during the next industrial revolution. ☐

b The fourth industrial revolution will be different from the previous ones. ☐

c People will adapt to the fourth industrial revolution and find new ways to cope and survive. ☐

d There will be huge job losses at the beginning of the fourth industrial revolution. ☐

e Education and training will open up new job opportunities. ☐

VOCABULARY BUILDING

A Complete the sentences using the correct form of the words and phrases in the box.

carry out	civilian	drawbacks
humanitarian	pose a hazard	surveillance

1 The misuse of technology _____ to everybody.

2 Remote-controlled devices, such as drones, can be used for _____ .

3 There are many ways in which technology can be used alongside _____ aid workers to help save lives.

4 Drones are not just used by the military nowadays; small ones are becoming popular among _____ .

5 New technology usually comes with both benefits and _____ .

6 Robots are getting better and better at _____ complex tasks efficiently.

B The phrasal verb *carry out* is often used with the following nouns. Complete the sentences using the words in the box.

attack	mission	orders	research	tasks

1 I carried out my boss's _____ , even though I didn't agree with them.

2 The alert soldier was able to prevent the enemy from carrying out their _____ on the base.

3 The team carried out their rescue _____ successfully—they found all five missing people, and none of them were hurt.

4 His job involves carrying out routine _____ in the office, such as photocopying.

5 A lot of life-saving _____ has been carried out in that lab.

A salamander-like robot. Biomimetics draws inspiration from nature to overcome human limitations.

9D
TED PLAYLIST

A ROBOT THAT FLIES LIKE A BIRD

There are many robots that are able to fly—but none have been able to fly like a real bird. That is, until Markus Fischer and his team built SmartBird, the first ultralight robot capable of flying like a real bird. In this talk, he demonstrates the amazing robot bird and explains how his team's work can help to create more efficient designs for industry.

A ROBOT THAT RUNS AND SWIMS LIKE A SALAMANDER

Auke Ijspeert works at the intersection of robotics, biology, and neuroscience. He designs biorobots: machines modeled after real animals. In this talk, Ijspeert demonstrates some of his biorobots and explains how they facilitate a better understanding of our own biology—for example, by unlocking previously unknown secrets of the spinal cord.

THESE ROBOTS COME TO THE RESCUE AFTER A DISASTER

Robin Murphy builds robots that fly, tunnel, swim, and crawl through disaster scenes, helping firefighters and rescue workers save more lives quickly and safely. In this talk, Murphy shows how robots can do tasks no human or animal could. He explains how robots were crucial to the rescue work during the World Trade Center attack and the Fukushima Daiichi nuclear disaster.

A What do all three TED Talks have in common?

   a They feature robots that can help humans in dangerous situations.

   b They explain how robots can further our understanding of animals.

   c They show how robots can help us in a variety of ways.

B Answer the questions.

   1 Which speakers modeled their robots on real animals?

   _____

   2 Name one way that biorobots are beneficial to humans.

   _____

   3 What are two advantages of using robots during disasters?

   _____

C Decide which talk you most want to watch. Watch it online at www.ted.com.

9E

WRITING Discussing the applications of a technology

A Read the sample writing passage about the applications of drone technology.

State your opinion. —— Personally, I think drones have many uses. Here, I want to focus on just two areas.

Firstly, remote-controlled devices such as drones can help save lives in natural disasters—they can get to places no human can go and provide information about survivors. In the future, they may even be able to carry the survivors to safety.

Secondly, drones can provide important information about the environment. They can measure the amount of carbon dioxide in the atmosphere and take photos and videos that show global warming, for example. This information is vital for humans to help us tackle serious issues like climate change.

Provide reasons and specific examples.

Make sure you have a conclusion. —— It's important to remember that drone technology already exists, and if we try to prevent its development, we are destined to fail. It is better to accept the technology and use it for good. I believe that we should continue drone research and development. I am certain the benefits outweigh the disadvantages.

B Write about how super-intelligent robots will change human lives. Answer the questions to plan your passage.

1 What is your opinion about super-intelligent robots? Should we develop them?

2 What are your reasons for your opinion?

3 What are your examples to support your reasons?

4 How will super-intelligent robots change people's lives? What is your conclusion?

C Now write your passage. Then complete the checklist below.

☐ Did you clearly state your opinion? ☐ Did you use correct spelling and punctuation?

☐ Did you provide several reasons and examples? ☐ Did you use some new words from this unit?

10 Connections

10A

VOCABULARY Collocations with *listen*

Which words or expressions best describe the way you would listen in the situations below?
Circle the best answer.

1 You are taking an exam and the examiner is explaining the procedure.

   a carefully   **b** politely

2 A close friend is telling you about an illness he's been suffering from.

   a patiently   **b** sympathetically

3 You are listening to an interview with a celebrity you really like.

   a anxiously   **b** with great interest

4 Your teacher is reading out the results of an important test that you and your classmates took.

   a anxiously   **b** politely

5 A friend is giving you some advice about a personal issue.

   a patiently   **b** thoughtfully

LISTENING Mediation

A ▶ **10.1** Listen to a conversation between friends. Which statement best describes the situation?

   a Their friend, Mike, is having problems at work and needs their help.

   b The woman wants some advice from their friends about a problem she's having.

   c They are too busy to help their friends Mike and Nikki.

B ▶ **10.1** Listen again. Match the sentence halves.

1 The woman said Mike was distracted   ○   ○ **a** because he kept getting messages on his phone.

2 The man was surprised Mike was distracted   ○   ○ **b** because she's a good listener.

3 The woman decided to talk to Nikki   ○   ○ **c** because he's usually a good listener.

4 The man thinks it's a good idea   ○   ○ **d** because she knows the situation and is a good friend.

COMMUNICATION Staying focused

A Circle the best response.

1 You didn't seem to be listening to the lecture. What was the problem?

    a My mind kept wandering. I'm worried about my exam results.

    b I can't remember what he was talking about.

2 It's so hard to concentrate in these meetings. How do you manage it?

    a He wasn't speaking clearly so nobody could hear him.

    b Well, I try to take notes.

3 All these message alerts on my phone are so distracting.

    a I prefer texting to making calls.

    b Yes, they make it really hard to focus on the lecture.

4 Do you think you're a good listener?

    a Yes, I think you usually listen patiently.

    b I guess it depends on who's talking and what it's about.

B Answer the questions using your own words.

1 Do you easily get distracted? If so, by what?

_____

2 Are you good at listening carefully? Why or why not?

_____

3 How do you stay focused during a class presentation?

_____

10B

LANGUAGE FOCUS Learning to listen

A Match the direct speech to the indirect speech statements.

1 "This is really interesting." ○   ○ **a** She said that the lecture was fascinating.

2 "You'll need to finish this exam by midday." ○   ○ **b** The examiner told us that we would need to finish the listening test by 12:00 p.m.

3 "Don't forget to record the presentation at 12:00 p.m." ○   ○ **c** They said they couldn't hear me because the mic wasn't functioning.

4 "We can't hear anything—the mic isn't working." ○   ○ **d** She said that he would have to use the mic because it was really loud in there.

5 "I think you'll have to use the mic—it's really noisy in here." ○   ○ **e** He reminded me to record the midday presentation.

B ▶ **10.2** Listen to each question or statement. Use the prompts to report what each speaker said.

1 He asked Chris _____ .

2 She promised _____ .

3 They said _____ .

4 She told Kyle _____ .

C Write the indirect speech statement.

1 "Listen quietly to what I am going to say."

_____

2 "I promise I won't get distracted and I'll listen carefully."

_____

3 "We're sorry we're late. There was an accident on the way and we were delayed."

_____

4 "Don't be late for the presentation, Andy!"

_____

5 "Karen, please hand in your homework tomorrow."

_____

LISTENING FOCUS Emphatic stress

A ▶ **10.3** Notice how the speaker stresses particular words to emphasize his point. Listen and repeat what you hear.

I want every student to listen **in silence**.

She listened to my complaint, but **not sympathetically**.

But you **promised** you would help me!

B ▶ **10.4** Underline the words that you think should be stressed. Then listen and check your answers.

1 That was a terrible movie.

2 I really enjoyed that lecture.

3 Don't you think that was a difficult test?

4 I highly recommend you hire him. He's a very good worker.

5 She's a rude child!

C ▶ **10.5** Listen to the statements. Circle the best response based on where the stress is placed in each statement.

1 a No, she gave a presentation on listening skills.   **b** No, Helen gave the presentation.

2 a Exactly. It wasn't the waiter's fault.   **b** Me neither. Tim's not usually like that.

3 a Peter was most affected by the mistake.   **b** Paul should be the one to apologize.

4 a No, I think he handles inventory.   **b** Jessica handles invoices these days.

10C

READING

Read the passage and answer the questions.

1   In 1987, American radio producer David Isay had an idea: Why not build a collection of interviews for people to listen to in the future—an oral history for future generations? In 2003, with the opening of a small booth in New York City's Grand Central Station, StoryCorps was born. "I had no idea if it would work, but from the very beginning, it did," says Isay. "People treated the experience with incredible respect, and amazing conversations happened inside."

2   StoryCorps interviews usually take place between two people who know and care about each other. A trained StoryCorps facilitator guides participants through the interview process. At the end of each 40-minute recording session, participants receive a free CD of their interview, or they can listen to it on the StoryCorps website. Today, there are several StoryCorps booths (called StoryBooths) throughout the United States. StoryCorps also has a mobile booth that travels across the country, recording stories in various cities. Recently, StoryCorps developed a free app that allows users to record stories on a smartphone. The app provides a do-it-yourself guide on how to prepare interview questions and set up the right recording environment. Users can then upload their interviews to the StoryCorps website.

3   Today, StoryCorps has the world's largest collection of real stories told by real people. In total, over 100,000 people have recorded interviews—all of which are highly personal—and millions listen to its weekly radio broadcasts and visit its website. Listeners regularly report crying when they hear StoryCorps stories. According to Isay, this is because "you're hearing something authentic and pure at this moment, when sometimes it's hard to tell what's real and what's an advertisement."

4   Isay's plan is to expand StoryCorps all over the world, as he believes that everyone has a story the world needs to hear. He explains, "Every day, people come up to me and say, 'I wish I had interviewed my father or my grandmother or my brother, but I waited too long.' Now, no one has to wait anymore."

Leslie Williams and her father, George Linker, interview each other in a StoryCorps Mobile Booth in Charlotte, North Carolina.

A What is the passage mainly about?

    a how StoryCorps changed David Isay's life

    b how David Isay came to create StoryCorps

    c what StoryCorps is and why it was created

B Answer the questions.

    1 What were people's reactions to the first StoryCorps booth in Grand Central Station?

    _____

    2 What does Isay mean by this statement: "… you're hearing something authentic and pure at this moment, when sometimes it's hard to tell what's real and what's an advertisement."

    _____

    3 Why do you think people cry when they listen to StoryCorps stories?

    _____

    4 Why do you think StoryCorps is such a success?

    _____

LISTENING

A ▶ **10.6** Listen. Which sentence best summarizes the talk?

    a By avoiding certain habits when we talk, we can become better speakers and influence the way people listen to us.

    b There are many reasons why it is hard to listen, including the distractions of modern technology and speakers' bad habits.

    c A lot of people tend to speak negatively or complain about others, and these are unpleasant habits we should all try to avoid.

B ▶ **10.6** Listen again. Check [✓] the habits that the speaker mentions.

    a gossiping about other people   ☐

    b finding faults   ☐

    c talking negatively   ☐

    d complaining about everything   ☐

    e making excuses for one's own actions   ☐

    f exaggerating everything   ☐

    g repeating everything several times   ☐

C **CRITICAL THINKING** Do you think you have good listening skills? Which points from the talk do you need to improve on?

_____

_____

VOCABULARY BUILDING

A Complete the sentences using the correct form of the words in the box.

disruptive	enhance	overestimate	pioneer	rapport

1 The pilot _____ the length of the runway, and the plane crashed into the sea.

2 Being interrupted by a phone call or message is usually quite _____ to our work.

3 If you are able to listen carefully and sympathetically, it helps build _____ with your colleagues.

4 Learning how to use your voice effectively _____ the delivery of your message.

5 Steve Jobs was a(n) _____ of the personal computer revolution.

B Complete the sentences using the correct form of the words in the box.

disapprove	discourage	discriminate	disappointed	dislike

1 It is wrong to _____ against people because of their race or gender.

2 Her mother really _____ of her gossiping.

3 I studied so hard and should have done better. I'm so _____ with my performance.

4 I'm not surprised you _____ him. He keeps blaming other people for his own mistakes.

5 She probably won't win the contest, but it's good to try. I don't think you should _____ her.

To be a better listener, practice active listening. Restate or paraphrase what you have heard to make sure you've understood the message correctly.

10D

TED PLAYLIST

People are easily distracted. It's important to communicate in ways that engage their attention.

HOW TO SPEAK SO THAT PEOPLE WANT TO LISTEN

Have you ever felt like you're talking, but nobody is listening? Do you want to be a powerful speaker that people will want to listen to? In this talk, Julian Treasure presents the seven deadly sins of speaking and then demonstrates the how-tos of powerful speaking—from useful vocal exercises to tips on how to speak with empathy.

EVERYONE AROUND YOU HAS A STORY THE WORLD NEEDS TO HEAR

In this talk, we learn how David Isay founded StoryCorps, the largest collection of human voices ever recorded. Isay's intention was to create a quiet place where a person could honor someone by listening to their story. Isay also shares his future vision: to take this idea global, and collect stories from around the world.

WANT TO HELP SOMEONE? SHUT UP AND LISTEN!

Development expert Ernesto Sirolli describes his first experience of aid work in Africa in the 1970s, and why it was ineffective. He emphasizes the importance of listening, and proposes that the first step for any aid worker is to listen to the people they're trying to help. His advice on what works will help any entrepreneur.

A What is each TED Talk about? Match the descriptions with the speakers.

1 listening carefully ○   ○ **a** David Isay

2 collecting personal conversations ○   ○ **b** Ernesto Sirolli

3 speaking to be heard ○   ○ **c** Julian Treasure

B Which speaker most likely said the following? Circle the best answer.

1 "There are a number of habits that we need to move away from."

  a David Isay   **b** Ernesto Sirolli   **c** Julian Treasure

2 "You sit across from, say, your grandfather for close to an hour and you listen and you talk."

  a David Isay   **b** Ernesto Sirolli   **c** Julian Treasure

3 "And what we do, we become friends, and we find out what that person wants to do."

  a David Isay   **b** Ernesto Sirolli   **c** Julian Treasure

C Decide which talk you most want to watch. Watch it online at www.ted.com.

WRITING A survey report

A Read the sample writing passage about the results of a survey on listening skills.

In the first line, summarize the results of the survey. ——The survey indicated that I am generally not a very good listener. While I have some good listening habits, such as making physical gestures to show that I'm listening and making eye contact with the speaker, I also have quite a few habits that are not so good.

For example, I usually check my phone if I get a message, and often take a moment to reply. Also, I am not very patient—I often interrupt if I don't agree with the person I'm talking with, and I think I form opinions very quickly about what the person is saying—often before they have finished speaking.

Give some specific examples to illustrate your points.

Describe what you think good listening habits are. I think that a good listener is someone who pays close attention to the speaker, listens carefully, and is aware of their body language. A good listener also waits for the speaker to finish and doesn't interrupt often. These are all things I intend to do in the future to become a better and more conscious listener.

Provide a concluding statement.

B Write a passage that summarizes your survey results and what it says about your listening habits. Answer the questions to plan your passage.

1 What is the general result of the survey?

2 What specific examples can you give?

3 What are some habits of good listeners?

C Now write your passage. Then complete the checklist below.

☐ Did you use correct spelling and punctuation?

☐ Did you describe some listening habits you think are good?

☐ Did you use some new words from this unit?

☐ Did you provide reasons and give specific examples?

11 Life in the Slow Lane

11A

VOCABULARY Slowing down

Complete the sentences using the words in the box.

appreciation	juggle	leisurely	meaningful	mindful	restore

1 A weekend surrounded by nature can help _____ your energy.

2 It takes time to form a(n) _____ relationship.

3 Being able to chat over a(n) _____ meal is one of life's simple pleasures.

4 It's tough for many people to _____ a career and a family.

5 When someone has done something nice for you, you should show your _____ .

6 If you are constantly rushing through life, it's hard to be _____ of where you are.

LISTENING Living in the present

A ▶ 11.1 Listen to a briefing by a camp leader. Which of these best describes the group of campers?

    a retirees   **b** working adults   **c** teenagers

B ▶ 11.1 Listen again. Circle the best answers.

1 What is the purpose of this camp?

    a building business networks

    b learning to eat healthily

    c slowing down to enjoy life

2 What does the speaker mean by "... talking about work is taboo here"?

    a It is forbidden.   **b** It is encouraged.   **c** It is allowed.

3 Which of these is **not** a rule at the camp?

    a No smoking or drinking.

    b Try to build business networks with other campers.

    c No gadgets during camp hours.

COMMUNICATION Leading a slower-paced life

Circle the best response.

1 Aren't you going away for the weekend on a retreat?

    a Yes, and I'm really looking forward to it. Work has been crazy.

    b Yes, I think a retreat would be great. I'd love to go on one.

2 I really need to get away from the city this weekend. Shall we go to the coast?

    a Sure. Being around water always makes me happier.

    b That's a great idea. I love the smell of the forest.

3 Are you looking forward to your hiking trip in the mountains?

    a Shall we? I'd definitely like to take things easy for a while.

    b Absolutely. It'll be great to slow down and disconnect.

4 What did Emily think of the yoga classes?

    a She said it was a great way to unwind.

    b That would be a great way to relax.

LANGUAGE FOCUS Multitasking versus monotasking

A Complete the sentences using the phrases in the box.

a large number	a little bit of	a lot of	every time

1 He's very health conscious so he only takes _____ sugar with his tea.

2 Researchers have discovered that _____ we receive a text message, the brain releases dopamine.

3 There is _____ concern about people who use their phones while driving—it's a serious problem.

4 In the last few years, more and more young people have become addicted to social media—it's now _____ .

B Circle the correct words. If no article is necessary, circle **x**.

1 She is (**the / an**) expert on (**the / x**) brain and how it deals with tasks.

2 When you are in (**a / the**) stressful situation, (**the / a**) body releases cortisol, a stress hormone.

3 Amy usually likes to unwind on (**the / x**) weekend and go for (**a / x**) hikes in the mountains.

4 I think that living in (**a / the**) countryside is much healthier than living in (**a / x**) city.

C Correct the mistakes in the sentences.

1 Pace of life today is much faster than it was 30 years ago.

2 The increasing number of the people like to disconnect and go tech-free at times.

3 Spending the day or two in nature is the great way to unwind.

4 Without an Internet, life and the work would be very different.

5 Jun has the large number of urgent emails to respond to.

LISTENING FOCUS Articles *a*, *an*, *the*

A ▶ **11.2** Articles (*a*, *an*, *the*) are often unstressed in a sentence and can be difficult to hear. Listen and repeat what you hear.

Noise and lots of distractions take **a** toll on **the** brain.

An increasing number of people are looking for **a** slower pace of life.

The email that I wrote today was **a** long and complicated one.

I often work in **the** evening if I have **an** urgent deadline.

B ▶ **11.3** Listen. Circle the sentence you hear. What is the difference in meaning between each pair?

1 a There was a hair on the floor.   **b** There was hair on the floor.

2 a I heard a noise coming from downstairs.   **b** I heard noise coming from downstairs.

3 a There was a glass on the kitchen table.   **b** There was glass on the kitchen table.

4 a How's the business?   **b** How's business?

5 a Is there a room for me?   **b** Is there room for me?

C ▶ **11.4** Listen. Complete the sentences with the words you hear.

1 I'm taking _____ to the countryside this weekend.

2 I need to get away from _____ for a few days.

3 Spending time at _____ helps me relax.

4 It'll be good to take things easy for _____ .

5 I've booked a room in _____ .

READING

Read the passage and answer the questions.

1   Chef Salvatore Toscano used to manage an American-style restaurant in Florence, Italy. He spent his days preparing and serving hamburgers—a symbol of fast food around the world. Then, he left all that behind and opened a new, different type of restaurant. He now cooks Slow Food, using fresh local produce, and the results are delicious.

The Slow Food movement aims to prevent the disappearance of local food cultures and traditions.

2   The Slow Food movement began in Italy in the 1980s—a reaction to the introduction of fast food. The aim of Slow Food is to preserve regional food traditions and encourage the use of local, sustainably farmed products that are prepared and eaten in a leisurely way. The Slow Food movement has had tremendous success in Italy, and has since gone international. The movement has more than 100,000 members in over 150 countries worldwide.

3   The Slow Food movement is not limited to the kitchen, either. It also encourages the value of taking time to enjoy dining. Chef Toscano makes sure that he finds the time to come out of his kitchen and talk to his customers to ask them how they enjoyed the food. This behavior is often rare in the fast-paced modern world, and it serves as a reminder that dining "slow" can be an enjoyable experience for everyone.

4   Another supporter of Slow Food, Italian farmer Luciano Bertini, sums up the importance of the movement. According to him, it's about making sure that everything in the world doesn't become exactly the same and that the world doesn't become bland and boring. "From Singapore to Macau," he says, "in New York and Rome, you always find the same pizza, the same hamburgers. Slow Food doesn't want this. Slow Food wants the specialness of every product to be respected."

5   The success of Slow Food has since inspired the Slow Movement, which expands the idea to all aspects of life including education, travel, and work. Today, the concept is often referred to as just Slow Living, an idea that Chef Toscano has also embraced. "It means taking the time," he says, "finding the rhythm that lets you live more calmly in a lot of ways, starting, of course, with what you eat."

A What is the best title for the passage?

   a The Rise of Fast Food in Italy   **b** How to Cook Slow Food   **c** From Fast Food to Slow Food

B Circle **T** for true, **F** for false, or **NG** for not given.

1 Chef Toscano is a champion of the Slow Food movement.	**T**	**F**	**NG**
2 The Slow Food movement began in the 1980s.	**T**	**F**	**NG**
3 Slow Food is about preserving food traditions.	**T**	**F**	**NG**
4 The Slow Food movement has many members in New York.	**T**	**F**	**NG**
5 Chef Toscano takes the time to build relationships with his customers.	**T**	**F**	**NG**
6 The Slow Food movement was inspired by the Slow Movement.	**T**	**F**	**NG**

LISTENING

A ▶ **11.5** Listen. Which sentence best summarizes the talk?

   a Jeonju, an official Slow City south of Seoul, supports its traditions and local environment.

   b Slow cities are beginning to appear in Asia, and Hanok Village in South Korea, is one example.

   c The Slow City movement's goal is to boost tourism in Asian cities.

B ▶ **11.5** Listen again. Answer the questions.

   1 What is the purpose of the Slow City movement?

      To encourage cities to support their _____

      _____

      _____

   2 Why was Jeonju certified as a Slow City?

      The award was in recognition of its efforts to _____

      _____

      _____

   3 Has the Slow City award benefited Jeonju? If so, how?

      Since receiving the award, there has been _____

      _____

      _____

   4 Why is the Slow City movement gaining popularity in Asian countries?

      _____

C **CRITICAL THINKING** Circle the statement you most agree with. Give a reason for your answer.

   a The Slow City movement is an attempt to counteract the effects of globalization.

   b The Slow City movement's increasing popularity around the world is a good thing.

   c European countries are best at appreciating the values of the Slow Movement.

      Reason: _____

VOCABULARY BUILDING

A Complete the sentences using the words in the box.

addiction	cognitive	evolved	intuitively	therapy

1 Injury to the brain can damage a person's _____ functions.

2 Humans _____ in nature, which is perhaps why we feel comfortable in natural surroundings.

3 There are a large number of people suffering from social media _____.

4 Meditation can be a useful form of _____, and there are no side effects.

5 We know _____ that being surrounded by nature is beneficial.

B What addiction is each person describing? Choose your answer from the box. Two are extra.

alcohol addiction	drug addiction	gambling addiction
gaming addiction	shopping addiction	

1 "It was a beautiful designer bag last week. This weekend, Joy's buying another two bags and some expensive shoes. Every weekend she buys a few more expensive items. Her credit card debt is now $15,000!"

_____

2 "Angie's teenage son was up till 3:30 a.m. He was trying to get to Level 50. It's the fifth time in a week that he went to bed after 3."

_____

3 "Tony had to sell his car six months ago to pay off his debts. But he couldn't stop his habit, and just last week he bet his entire house. He lost and now has to move out."

_____

A hanok, or traditional house, in Jeonju's Hanok Village—one of the eleven Slow Cities in South Korea.

11D

TED PLAYLIST

Studies have shown that meditation helps boost immunity, improve well-being, and sharpen the mind's focus.

In this talk, mindfulness expert Andy Puddicombe recommends we all take regular breaks from our restless minds. Puddicombe describes how, by just refreshing your mind for 10 minutes a day, you can become healthier and happier. It's a simple step to being mindful and experiencing the present moment.

Pico Iyer takes a look at the insights and clarity that come with taking time for stillness. In our world of constant movement and distraction, he shows the power of taking time for sitting still and reflecting, whether for a few minutes in a day or a few days every season.

What do we all have in common? The desire to be happy, says scholar and monk David Steindl-Rast. In this talk, Steindl-Rast suggests that happiness comes from gratitude. He explains how, if we can slow down and be grateful for the many small opportunities life gives us, we can learn to live gratefully and happily.

A Match each talk title to the correct speaker.

1 The Art of Stillness   ○   ○ **a** David Steindl-Rast

2 Want to Be Happy? Be Grateful   ○   ○ **b** Andy Puddicombe

3 All It Takes Is 10 Mindful Minutes ○   ○ **c** Pico Iyer

B Answer the questions.

1 According to Steindl-Rast, what is the one thing people have in common?

_____

2 What do Puddicombe's and Iyer's talks have in common?

_____

3 "And of course sitting still is how many of us get what we most crave and need in our accelerated lives, a break." Which speaker most likely said this?

_____

C Decide which talk you most want to watch. Watch it online at www.ted.com.

WRITING An advertisement

A Read the sample passage from an advertisement for a hiking organization that helps people get away from it all and slow down.

State what the organization is and what it does.

End with a conclusion that states the benefits of the activities.

> Do you feel stressed? Do you need an energy boost? Would you like to get away from it all, be surrounded by nature, and recharge your batteries? Then join us on one of our hiking trips.
>
> Here at JustHike, we organize <u>fantastic</u> hiking trips to beautiful places. Only have a day? No problem—take one of our many day trips. Or maybe you're looking for a longer trip? We have that covered, too. Choose from a range of hiking experiences, and add on exciting activities like white-water rafting if you're feeling adventurous. If you're looking for something more relaxed, we can take you to scenic mountains and put you up in a comfortable log cabin where you can sample delicious local food and drink.
>
> So what are you waiting for? Let JustHike take you on a hiking holiday that will restore your energy, reduce your stress, get you fitter, connect you with other people, and give you an experience you won't forget!

Use positive-sounding adjectives.

Say what kind of activities are available.

B Create an advertisement for an organization that encourages people to get away from their busy city lives. Answer the questions to plan your advertisement.

1 How can you grab people's attention?

2 What is the organization called? What does it do?

3 What kind of activities are available? What are the key details?

4 What are the benefits of doing the activities? How do they help people slow down?

C Now write your advertisement. Then complete the checklist below.

☐ Did you say what kind of activities are available?

☐ Did you use some new words and adjectives from this unit?

☐ Did you outline the benefits of the activities?

☐ Did you state what the organization is and what it does?

12 Make Yourself Heard

12A

VOCABULARY Voicing an opinion

A Complete the sentences using the correct form of the words in the box.

assert	clarify	conflict	persuade	resolve

1 As a manager, she really needs to _____ herself more.

2 The management began to take steps to _____ the company's problems.

3 The CEO asked her to _____ whether these were facts or just her opinions.

4 Whistleblowers who are company employees often face a(n) _____ of interest.

5 The board of directors _____ the CEO to do the right thing and resign.

B Answer the questions using your own words.

1 When was the last time you persuaded someone to do something? What was it?

_____

2 Give an example of a problem you or a friend had to resolve recently.

_____

LISTENING Standing up for your beliefs

A ▶ 12.1 Listen. Which statement best describes the speakers' situation?

a They are talking about a contract signing with a new business partner.

b They are discussing what to do about a colleague who wrongfully accepted some money.

c They are talking about the company's policy regarding accepting cash gifts.

B ▶ 12.1 Listen again. Circle the best answers.

1 How do the speakers feel about the situation?

   a They feel it's wrong.   **b** They think it's unfair.

2 Why is the woman worried?

   a Lewis's action could get them both in trouble.   **b** She wasn't appreciated for her efforts.

COMMUNICATION Managing conflict

Circle the best response.

1 I'm not sure what to do about my new team member. He's always late.

   a Have you tried talking to him about it?

   b Did you know that he often arrives late?

2 I never seem to get a chance to voice my opinion in meetings.

   a Do you find it easy to voice your opinion in front of strangers?

   b Maybe you should try to be more assertive.

3 The argument between the CEOs of our two companies seems never-ending.

   a Yes, I often argue with our company CEO.

   b Yes, I really hope they resolve the issue soon.

4 Why don't you tell the media what you found out about the business deal?

   a I'm afraid that if I do, I'll get fired immediately.

   b Have you tried letting the media know what you think?

LANGUAGE FOCUS Disasters that could have been prevented

A Circle the correct words.

1 If there (**was** / **hadn't been**) an earthquake, the village (**will still be** / **would still be**) standing.

2 If he (**hadn't fallen** / **didn't fall**) asleep on the job, the lab (**hadn't** / **wouldn't have**) burned down.

3 If you (**were** / **hadn't been**) texting, you (**wouldn't have** / **had**) crashed.

4 If we (**didn't sound** / **hadn't sounded**) the alarm, the rescuers (**didn't** / **wouldn't have**) known we were here!

5 If there (**hasn't been** / **hadn't been**) a tsunami, there (**won't have** / **wouldn't have**) been a leak at the power plant.

B Circle the best response.

1 Why did you tell your boss you were offered a bribe?

   a If I hadn't, it would have been wrong.

   b If I do, it will resolve the situation.

2 Why were you working so late on your homework last night? Did you finish it?

   a Yes. I wouldn't finish it if I didn't work so late.

   b Yes. I wouldn't have finished it if I hadn't worked so late.

3 Do you think I should talk to Mario about the problem with my computer?

   a Yes. If you do, he'll be able to help.

   b Yes. If you didn't, he would have helped.

C Rewrite the information below. The first example is given.

1 I voiced my opinion because I was right.
   If I hadn't been right, I wouldn't have voiced my opinion.

2 There was a big leak of classified documents. You now know the company's problems.
   If there hadn't _____

3 I believe in the power of real stories. That's why I became a journalist.
   If I didn't _____

4 They kept quiet about the wrongdoing. It's because they received threats.
   If they hadn't _____

5 She signed up for the skiing trip. She's joining us tomorrow.
   If she hadn't _____

LISTENING FOCUS Reduction of *have* with *would* and *wouldn't*

A ▶ **12.2** When talking about the imaginary past, the auxiliary verb *have* is often reduced. Listen and repeat what you hear.

I **would have** told you if I'd known how you felt.

I **would have** won if you hadn't cheated.

I **wouldn't have** complained if you hadn't mentioned it.

I **wouldn't have** passed the exam if I hadn't studied so hard.

B ▶ **12.3** Listen to the first half of each sentence and choose the most logical ending.

1 a … if you hadn't helped me.	**b** … if you hadn't been so noisy.
2 a … if my boss hadn't increased my pay.	**b** … if my boss had increased my pay.
3 a … if you hadn't told him.	**b** … if you'd told him.
4 a … if you hadn't done your homework.	**b** … if you'd done your homework.
5 a … if her interview hadn't gone so well.	**b** … if her interview hadn't gone so badly.

C ▶ **12.4** Listen. Complete the sentences using the words you hear.

1 They _____ gotten married if _____ love each other.

2 It _____ quicker if _____ a taxi.

3 She _____ come to the party if _____ her.

4 If it _____ so expensive, I _____ bought it.

5 If _____ about it, I _____ said something.

READING

Read the passage and answer the questions.

1 Since the beginning of the 21st century, there has been a horrifying increase in the number of elephants, rhinos, tigers, and other species killed by poachers. The illegal and often violent wildlife trade now threatens the very survival of not just these species, but also apes, pangolins, and several species of reptiles and birds. This trade is estimated to be worth up to $20 billion, the 4th largest illegal trade in the world. The criminal gangs that organize the trade are more sophisticated than ever before, and widespread

Chimpanzees have already disappeared from four African countries, and are nearing extinction in the rest.

corruption means that people who are aware of what is going on are reluctant to talk to anyone.

2 Up to now, it has been very difficult to detect wildlife crimes, but WildLeaks, a website launched in 2014, is shining a small ray of hope on this depressing picture. WildLeaks provides a safe and completely anonymous way of blowing the whistle on wildlife and forest crimes. Its targets are not low-level poachers but corrupt officials, traffickers, businessmen, and shipping companies at the top of the pyramid. Andrea Crosta, project leader, explains that WildLeaks is different from the similar-sounding WikiLeaks. Unlike the latter, information is not automatically leaked to the media—instead, it is analyzed and verified, and then the WildLeaks team of professionals decides on the best course of action. For example, the team may pass the information to trusted law enforcement officers, or carry out an investigation independently. However, "the goal is always to expose wildlife crimes and put the responsible individuals behind bars," clarifies Crosta.

3 The WildLeaks team is optimistic that the site can help make a difference and reduce wildlife crime. Crosta points out that although various hotlines exist for whistleblowers, these are set up by government agencies, whereas WildLeaks is politically neutral. He hopes and expects that with this knowledge, people will be much more comfortable informing WildLeaks of wildlife crime.

A What is the main purpose of the passage?

    a to highlight the scale of global wildlife crime trade

    b to describe how WildLeaks can help prevent wildlife crime

    c to explain the difference between WildLeaks and WikiLeaks

B Answer the questions.

    1 Why is the illegal wildlife trade such a widespread problem?

    _____

    2 How is WildLeaks different from WikiLeaks?

    _____

    _____

    3 Why do you think the WildLeaks team sometimes carries out an investigation independently?

    _____

LISTENING

A ▶ **12.5** Listen. Which sentence best summarizes the talk?

    a Websites like WildLeaks have many challenges to overcome before they can really make a difference.

    b The populations of elephants, tigers, and other species have been severely reduced by poachers.

    c The website WildLeaks is having a positive impact in stopping illegal wildlife trade.

B ▶ **12.5** Listen again. Circle **T** for true or **F** for false.

    1 The wildlife trade helps finance wars and fighting in certain countries.   **T**   **F**

    2 Information about wildlife criminals is kept confidential.   **T**   **F**

    3 There is a market for illegal animal products in the United States.   **T**   **F**

    4 In the elephant poaching tip-off, several top officials were named as suspects.   **T**   **F**

    5 200 years ago, there were 400,000 elephants—today there are only 20,000.   **T**   **F**

C **CRITICAL THINKING** Who do you think plays a bigger role in wildlife crimes: poachers, corrupt officials, or people who buy endangered animals? Give reasons for your answer.

_____

Reasons: _____

_____

VOCABULARY BUILDING

A Complete the sentences using the words in the box.

anonymous	classified	discredit
retaliate	unprecedented	wrongdoing

1 Many tip-offs provided to WildLeaks show clear examples of _____.

2 Releasing _____ documents to the public is a dangerous thing to do.

3 Organizations often _____ against people who try to harm them.

4 Whistleblowers often have to fight efforts made to _____ them.

5 The scale of wildlife destruction in the past few years is _____.

6 Most whistleblowers want to remain _____, because if people know their identity, it can put their lives at risk.

B Complete the sentences using the words in the box.

access	growth	level	number	opportunity

1 The fight against wildlife crime requires an unprecedented _____ of international cooperation.

2 WikiLeaks has given everybody unprecedented _____ to thousands of secret documents.

3 The anti-corruption president was supported by an unprecedented _____ of voters.

4 China has undergone unprecedented _____ in recent years.

5 The spread of smartphones and social media provides an unprecedented _____ for people to express themselves.

Easier access and the encroachment of people into the forests has led to increased hunting of orangutans.

12D

TED PLAYLIST

Malala Yousafzai is a Pakistani activist for female education and the youngest (ever) Nobel Prize laureate.

HERE'S HOW WE TAKE BACK THE INTERNET

In 2013, Edward Snowden leaked thousands of classified documents, sparking a global conversation about citizens' rights to privacy on the Internet. In this talk, Snowden speaks about surveillance and Internet freedom. He suggests we need to rethink the role of the Internet in our lives—and the laws that protect it. "Your rights matter," he says, "because you never know when you're going to need them."

MY DAUGHTER, MALALA

In this talk, Pakistani educator Ziauddin Yousafzai reminds us that women and men deserve equal opportunities. He tells stories from his own life and the life of his daughter, Malala, who he inspired to promote the rights of children to an education. Despite a Taliban attack on Malala in 2012, Yousafzai continues his fight to educate children in the developing world.

MY BATTLE TO EXPOSE GOVERNMENT CORRUPTION

Our leaders need to be held accountable, says journalist and freedom of information campaigner Heather Brooke. Brooke uncovered the British Parliamentary financial expenses scandal—a major political scandal that emerged in 2009. In this talk, Brooke urges us to ask our leaders questions, and to hold them responsible for giving answers.

A What do the TED Talks have in common?

a They feature people who stood up for what they believe in.

b They feature people who exposed political wrongdoing.

c They feature people who work to uncover corruption.

B Match each quote to the correct speaker.

1 "The data that I wanted to get my hands on were the expense receipts of members of Parliament." ○

○ **a** Heather Brooke

2 "Journalism is not a crime, communication is not a crime, and we should not be monitored in our everyday activities." ○

○ **b** Ziauddin Yousafzai

3 "I have five sisters, and none of them could go to school." ○

○ **c** Edward Snowden

C Decide which talk you most want to watch. Watch it online at www.ted.com.

WRITING An email

A Read the sample email to a CEO about the discovery of banned chemicals being used by the company and how the problem was handled.

Clarify the purpose of the email.
> Dear Mr. Smith,
> I am writing to update you about the discovery of the banned chemical in our products and the employee who discovered its use.

Explain the actions you have taken.
> This morning, I met the employee in order to persuade her not to talk to the media, as you requested. I convinced her that we were all unaware that the chemical was being used, and I promised that we would stop using it.

> As a result, the employee has agreed not to talk to anyone. However, she insists that we act immediately and that we also carry out an internal investigation to find out how we came to use the chemical and who was aware. I have agreed that we will do both things.
Explain the results of your actions.

Conclude with what the actions will mean.
> I am pleased, therefore, to be able to tell you that the problem will be resolved without any discredit to the company's reputation. I will keep you fully informed as we move forward.

Close the email.
> Best regards,
> Elaine Chang

B Imagine you're the CEO who received the above email. Write a reply to the email. Answer the questions to plan your email.

1 What is the purpose of your email?

2 Do you agree with the way the matter was handled?

3 Do you have any other suggestions to offer?

4 As the CEO, what are your future actions? What do you want to convey to your employees?

C Now write your email. Then complete the checklist below.

☐ Did you clearly state the purpose of the email?

☐ Did you describe the decisions you made and the actions to be taken?

☐ Did you use correct spelling and punctuation?

☐ Did you use some new words from this unit?

Audio Scripts

Unit 1

▶ 1.1

A: So what can I do for you today?

B: Well, doctor, I've been feeling very stressed lately. I'm tired all the time and don't have much appetite.

A: That's not good. Do you work long hours?

B: Yes, and I'm managing a project with a lot of tight deadlines.

A: That could be the reason. What are you doing to cope with all this stress?

B: Umm . . . I try to relax in the evening by watching TV, but it's hard. I get so many messages from work that I have to reply to.

A: Hmm. How about exercise? Do you do any?

B: Not really. I don't have time.

A: That's not good. It's important to get out and do some exercise. It's also a great way to relieve stress.

B: Okay. I'll try to find the time.

A: That's good. How about your sleeping habits? Do you get enough sleep?

B: To be honest, I don't. I go to sleep quite late and I have to get up very early.

A: No wonder you're tired all the time! You should balance work and rest. Aim to get at least 8 hours of sleep. And try not to use any gadgets one hour before bedtime.

B: That's going to be very hard to do. But what about my appetite? Do you think that's also related to the stress?

A: Yes, almost certainly. You could try meditating. It's proven to help you relax and reduce your stress levels.

B: I've heard about it, but I've never tried it before.

A: Well . . .

▶ 1.2

A: Do you think you can cope with stress?

B: Hmm. I think I generally handle stress well.

A: Okay. Do you enjoy working in an office or outdoors?

B: Oh, definitely outdoors. I hate being indoors for long periods.

A: And how about working with people? Would you like to help people in need?

B: Well, I guess I'd like to help people if I could. I enjoy being social.

A: Have you considered working in the healthcare industry?

B: Like a nurse or doctor? Umm, I think I'd prefer to do something more exciting, something requiring physical activity.

A: Hmm . . . How about the military?

B: No, I can't imagine being in the military. I don't mind the danger, but I don't like the idea of hurting other people.

A: Have you ever thought about a career as a firefighter?

B: Ah, now that's a good idea!

▶ **1.3** She expects to work overseas after she finishes college.; I really enjoy working with other people.; I can't imagine being in the Army, but maybe in the Air Force.; I'm coping with the stress quite well at the moment. But I'm not sure how long I can keep it up.

▶ **1.4** **1.** Hajime doesn't plan to do a Master's. He wants to do a Ph.D.; **2.** My parents always encouraged me to become a doctor.; **3.** My sister can't imagine having a desk job.; **4.** I considered doing a degree in Spanish, but I chose English in the end.

▶ **1.5** **1.** I'm not planning to travel overseas at the moment, but I will someday.; **2.** I enjoy being with people of course, but I prefer working on my own.; **3.** The interviewers told me they didn't want to hire me yet, but they'd call me if an opening came up.; **4.** I want to travel around the world now because I won't be able to once I settle down.

▶ **1.6** If you're like most people, you're not a fan of stress. Maybe you're interested in finding a job with low stress? If so, you should probably look for jobs which involve working on your own or helping other people, are not in the public eye, allow you some control over your schedule, and which don't have tight deadlines. Let's take a look at some of these occupations. Perhaps surprisingly, there are some relatively low-stress jobs that pay very well, which we'll focus on later.

One job that perhaps comes to mind when we think of low stress occupations is being a librarian. If you enjoy reading and have good organizational skills, this could be the job for you. A hairstylist's job satisfaction is often high and stress is low. Jewelers generally also have low levels of stress. If you'd prefer a manual job, you could consider becoming a forklift operator—working mostly on your own, it is one of the least stressful occupations.

If you want a reasonably low-stress job with a good salary, what are your choices? Unsurprisingly, the educational requirements are usually high. One option is to become a university professor. Full-time professors generally have flexible schedules as well as manageable workloads. You could consider being a scientist or mathematician, too. If you love stargazing, then a good choice would be astronomy.

Or perhaps you might want to consider being a software developer? They usually have flexible schedules and can work from home most of the time. Finally, if you are more interested in the arts, you may want to work as an art director—a job that involves creating the visual style and images in printed materials as well as on TV.

Do any of these choices sound like the job for you?

Unit 2

▶ **2.1**

A: That was a great movie. Amazing special effects in the battle scenes.

B: Yeah, they were fantastic. But the plot was a bit predictable. It was obvious that the hero would win.

A: Yeah, I guess. But heroes are supposed to win. They wouldn't make good role models if they lost.

B: I'm not sure the hero did make a good role model. All she did was fight. I lost count of all the people she killed.

A: What's wrong with that? She was fighting the bad guys. And there were a lot of them!

B: Yeah, but all that violence. What sort of message does that send to children? That we should sort out problems with violence?

A: It's only a movie. It's just entertainment. It's not real.

B: You don't think what goes on in movies has an influence on people?

A: No, I don't. We're hardly going to start shooting people just because we saw movie characters do it, are we?

B: Of course not. We're adults. But what about kids?

A: Kids these days are pretty smart. They know the difference between real life and movies.

B: I hope so . . . It was good entertainment, for sure, but I prefer more realistic stories. You know, where the characters are more complex. Where it's not all just good guys and bad guys.

A: But sometimes you just want an action movie with a good old hero. It makes you feel good and you forget about real-life problems.

B: Yeah. But I think often they use action and violence to make up for a weak plot. Give me a strong storyline and believable characters any day.

A: OK, well next time you get to choose the movie.

B: OK. Just don't complain if there isn't much action!

▶ **2.2** I saw a documentary that featured a really brave person.; I was inspired to volunteer after listening to her interview on TV.; Some studies have shown that playing video games improves the brain.; People who often spend time watching negative news on TV may become more pessimistic.

▶ **2.3** **1.** I was really inspired by the nature documentary.; **2.** The first three people to call up the hotline will win free movie tickets.; **3.** The study found that watching comedies caused people's blood pressure to become lower.; **4.** The program raised people's awareness of the risks of global warming.; **5.** I'm impressed by the way some celebrities use their fame to help people.; **6.** The rules are clear: You must be older than 18 to watch the movie.

▶ **2.4** **1.** What do you think of superheroes who have disabilities?; **2.** Do you think pop stars can make good role models?; **3.** Is social media a force for good?; **4.** What kind of movies do you find the most powerful?

▶ **2.5** Do video games have bad effects on children? There is a lot of debate on the topic, especially regarding violent games, but evidence suggests there *are* a number of ways in which video games are harmful to children.

Firstly, some studies show a correlation between playing violent games and aggressive thoughts and behaviors in children. And the effects are made worse if the game rewards players for behaving aggressively—some researchers claim that kids who regularly play violent games are more likely to be violent in real life and less empathetic. In many games, cooperation and non-violence are not options, so the children are taught bad values instead of having good role models as they develop. Some games also reinforce negative gender stereotypes, showing female characters to be weak and vulnerable.

There may be other harmful effects too. The addictive nature of games means that it's easy to play for too long. This can make a child socially isolated and have a negative impact on academic achievement, as well as on the child's health. And at least one study suggests that kids addicted to video games have higher levels of depression and anxiety. In addition, being immersed in a fantasy world for long periods can cause children to confuse fantasy with the real world. Furthermore, studies also indicate that although short-term concentration may be improved, long-term concentration, which is vital for academic success, may be damaged.

Although the debate continues regarding the possible harmful effects of video games, it seems clear that if we want our children to become well-adjusted and responsible adults, we should limit their exposure to violent games.

Unit 3

▶ **3.1** What are the most common goals and aspirations of college students after they graduate? A recent survey provides some answers. Nine in ten students said that their main priority for work and life was to be happy and to have a good work-life balance. Furthermore, 80 percent said they wanted to find a good job.

But what does a good job mean? Sixty-one percent indicated that they wanted a job with a good salary, while half said that finding a job that gave them enjoyment and satisfaction was vital. So, good pay and job satisfaction are two important factors when it comes to college students' goals. Perhaps related to these factors is the goal of obtaining post-graduate degrees. Nearly 40 percent said that they planned to continue their studies immediately after graduating.

But are students really ambitious? Not very, it seems. Only 11 percent said their main priority was to get to the top in their careers. And just 7 percent said they wanted to start their own businesses. One positive trend seems to be that students are increasingly altruistic. Thirty-one percent, nearly one in three, said that they wanted to be able to help the less fortunate, either through volunteering in their own time or through their jobs. Five years ago, this figure was one in four.

How about students' personal lives? What are their non-career goals? Well, perhaps unsurprisingly, nearly all students, 95 percent, said that finding a partner they could share their lives with was important. And seven in ten said they hoped to have children someday.

▶ **3.2**

A: How has your day been? Have you finished all ten homework questions?

B: I've done seven so far. The eighth is hard. I've been working on it for an hour already and I still haven't finished. How about you?

A: Well, I've been writing an essay for my English class since 8 o'clock. I've written the introduction and main part. I'm just about to start the conclusion.

B: Do you think you'll finish tonight?

A: Hmm . . . I've been working pretty fast, so I think so. How about you?

B: I certainly hope so. I've already made plans to go out later.

▶ **3.3** Most emerging economies have been doing well for the past few years.; How long has the population been shrinking?; Their charity has been helping the poor in the neighborhood since 2005.; Where have the non-profit organizations been doing most of their work?; With the trend for healthy food, people haven't been spending as much on fast food.

▶ **3.4** **1.** Disruptive tech has been introduced in many different areas.; **2.** The statistics show that there has been an increase in poverty.; **3.** A lower birthrate has been found to be the key to greater prosperity.; **4.** For the last few years, people all over the world have been using smartphones to access the Internet.; **5.** Have you been following his webinar on creative marketing strategies?; **6.** Has there been a breakthrough in her research? I saw her celebrating with her friends!

▶ **3.5** **1.** How long have you been thinking of doing a Ph.D.?; **2.** Have incomes in your countries been getting higher?; **3.** Why do you think so many people have been studying IT in the last five or ten years?; **4.** How have spending habits changed over the last 10 years?

▶ **3.6** In recent years, there has been increasing debate about the limitations of using GDP to measure a country's progress. According to David Cameron, the former British prime minister, ". . . there's more to life than money, and it's time we focused not just on GDP, but on GWB—general well-being."

But what really is the best way to measure well-being and happiness? One tiny mountainous country in the Himalayas, between India and China, may have the answer. Unlike other countries, Bhutan uses Gross National Happiness, or GNH, to measure its prosperity and what it has accomplished. The GNH index factors in preservation of the culture, good government, fair social development, and protection of the environment. To that end, the country has banned logging exports and has promised to keep 60 percent of its land forested forever.

In the last 25 years, life expectancy has doubled, infrastructure has been greatly improved, and nearly every child now attends primary school. It is true that Bhutan remains a very poor country, with many of its citizens still without electricity and struggling to live on just a few dollars a day. However, it has become clear that all the countries of the world cannot continue to focus their priorities on growth and increased consumption indefinitely—our resources are not endless and we only have one planet to support us.

This reality has helped give rise to a trend of measuring happiness and well-being, and we now have the World Happiness Report and the Happy Planet Index. So as we face the enormous challenges of climate change, environmental destruction, and social inequality, perhaps Bhutan's strong focus on well-being and sustainability, rather than its production of goods, shows us a better and fairer path and more altruistic aspirations.

Unit 4

▶ **4.1**

A: Have you ever stretched the truth at work?

B: Yeah, and I really regretted it.

A: Why, what happened?

B: Well, during the interview for my last job, I was asked about my language skills. The job involved travel around Asia and they needed someone who could speak more than one language.

A: You speak some Korean and Japanese, don't you?

B: Yes, and my Japanese is quite good, but my Korean is pretty basic. Anyway, I told them that my Japanese and Korean were both pretty fluent. And I got the job.

A: So far so good.

B: Mm. Well, not long into the job, I was asked to go to Korea on a business trip. I was excited and did a lot of preparation for the trip. And at first it all went well.

A: Oh yeah?

B: Yeah. We met the client at our office for an initial chat. Then we set up a meeting for the next day at the client's office. They wanted me to present to a group of managers.

A: I think I know what's coming.

B: Ha, Yeah. When I got there, just before I began, my boss told me that I had to present in Korean as some of the managers didn't speak good English. I was horrified. I'd forgotten all about the interview. I started to panic.

A: Oh no!

B: Well, I began but it was obvious that my Korean was way too basic, and I had to stop after a minute and switch to English. It was absolutely awful!

A: I can imagine. What happened afterwards?

B: My boss was furious. He said we'd lost face. And we lost the deal. I nearly lost my job over it.

A: I guess you're lucky you didn't.

B: Yeah, I guess. So I'm pretty careful never to stretch the truth now.

▶ **4.2** She must have been happy about that.; That could have been her at the door.; You might have eaten too much.; He can't have known about it.

▶ **4.3** **1.** I think you must have been mistaken.; **2.** She might become the president.; **3.** He could have come to the party alone.; **4.** They can't have many friends at school.

▶ **4.4** **1.** I think he might have tried to call you earlier.; **2.** With a bit more luck, he could have become famous.; **3.** The robbers must have come in through the back door.; **4.** That can't be the correct answer.

▶ **4.5**

A: Hi there! How was Andy's big presentation? Did it go well?

B: Hmm. It was okay, but he could have done a better job.

A: In what way?

B: Well, his delivery wasn't good. He mumbled quite a lot and lost his place a few times. He looked pretty nervous. And some of his slides were a bit difficult to understand.

A: That's not good. You gave him your opinion afterwards?

B: Um, actually, I said it was fine. It was his first big presentation so I wanted to boost his confidence.

A: But it wasn't fine. How is he is going to learn if you don't tell him the truth? He's an adult. I'm sure he can cope with some criticism.

B: I'm not sure. He's quite sensitive. With some people, we need to bend the truth a bit. Being too honest can make things worse.

A: I don't agree. It's simple. Being honest is always better. You can still be supportive.

B: Yeah, but right now I think it might be better to avoid criticizing him. He's had some problems recently, and I don't want him to take my feedback the wrong way. When the time is right, I'll talk to him.

A: I'd do it soon. What if other colleagues talk about it? He may ask you why you didn't mention it.

B: Hmm. Yes. That's a point.

A: Just do it professionally. I'm sure he'll appreciate the advice.

B: Maybe. But we're not all thick-skinned like you!

Unit 5

▶ **5.1** What words come to mind when you think of running a marathon? Endurance? Suffering? The ultimate challenge?

Many people regard running a marathon as being one of the toughest things a person can do, and it is clearly not an easy task to run 42 kilometers at any speed. Top marathon runners can maintain a speed of an incredible 20 kilometers an hour. One of the fastest marathon runners in the world is a man called Geoffrey Mutai. He set a record in 2011 for running the Boston Marathon in two hours and three minutes, the fastest ever.

But if you ask Mutai about suffering and endurance, he would not talk about running. Mutai was born into a large and very poor family in Kenya, who lived in a very simple home without electricity. The eldest of 11 children, he had to leave school after finishing elementary school. He started to train when he was 13, although he couldn't even afford shoes at the time. To help his family, he had to take on some very difficult, physically demanding jobs, such as working in a quarry, on a farm, and cutting down trees.

For Mutai, the really hard part was getting to his first race. He finally reached his goal of taking part in his first marathon in 2007, and came second. A year later, he won the Monaco Marathon and a prize of 4,000 euros. Fourteen years after he began training, he had become a top professional athlete. The difficult life experiences he had faced helped him become one of the fastest long-distance runners on the planet.

▶ **5.2** By midday, I had already finished two reports.; He had been studying filmmaking for several years.; How many records had she set by the time she was 22?; Had he been running for long before he won the race?

▶ **5.3** **1.** He had been reading a lot but he hadn't started writing his report.; **2.** How many milestones had he reached by the time he retired?; **3.** He had already become a millionaire before he graduated from college.; **4.** Had she been training for the Olympics for a long time?; **5.** By the time he turned 40, he had already been living in Greece for 15 years.

▶ **5.4** **1.** Had you been around, could you have seen the robbery from your house?; **2.** She'd asked me to inform you of the change in time, but I forgot.; **3.** They'd traveled to Italy before, so they were familiar with the place.; **4.** We'd already looked all over the park, but still couldn't find the missing dog.

▶ **5.5** It's no secret that the key to achieving one's goals and dreams is the ability to persevere and not give up in the face of challenges. Entrepreneurs, professional athletes, and successful people everywhere know this, from direct experience. What is it that gives them the power to keep going? Let's look at a few simple but important tips that may help you as you work toward realizing your dreams.

First, realize that setbacks are not really setbacks in the negative sense. Most successful people will tell you that some of the most important lessons they have learned arose when things went wrong. Setbacks are often great opportunities to learn valuable lessons—stepping stones to success.

Second, and related to how you regard setbacks, accept that there will never be a smooth path to success. Learn to accept that things won't go as you planned, and stay optimistic. If you do that, you will increase your chances of success.

Third, remember you are human—we all need to relax and take a break from work regularly. This doesn't only help us regain focus; research suggests that when we allow our minds to relax we are often at our most creative. Do a bit of exercise, have a cup of tea, meditate for a while. All are great ways to recharge the mind.

Finally, be content with whatever stage you are at right now. Life is full of goals, dreams, and challenges, and it's all happening now. Stay in the present and enjoy what you are doing, rather than worrying about the next stage.

So be calm, positive, and focused on the present, and let yourself relax from time to time. There'll always be another goal just around the corner.

Unit 6

▶ **6.1** The Internet is changing the way ordinary people do philanthropy. Until recently, if we wanted to donate our money to help people in low-income countries, pretty much our only option was to contribute to the funds of an NGO or charity working in a particular field. Rarely did we get to direct precisely how our $20 would be spent. But donation is getting specific, and it's getting personal—and it's thanks in part to the rise of crowdfunding.

Crowdfunding, which means getting funding for a specific goal from a large number of people or the general public, is not a new concept. In 1885, the Statue of Liberty's pedestal was famously crowdfunded by more than 160,000 donors. But the Internet has brought new scale and reach to the challenge of crowdfunding, moving beyond the readership of the 1885 New York World newspaper, and out into every corner of the world.

Today's crowdfunding is driven by technology. It combines the increasing access and reach of the Internet and the connecting powers of social media to inspire and motivate young fundraisers to donate—and in particular, to donate to very specific, personally-chosen causes. People are logging onto websites like KickStarter, identifying creative projects with which they feel a connection, and then with a few clicks, sending their money to help finance these initiatives. Others are logging onto websites like Kiva and scrolling through pitches to contribute their money to loans that will help specific people in low-income brackets build and grow their businesses. They donate knowing that their money isn't going into a big pot of funds, but directly to a person they have chosen to help, and they get updates on how it is spent.

Crowdfunding is inspiring a new generation of donors today. It may or may not emerge as a key future funding strategy, but it is already reaching some of the people who need help most.

▶ **6.2** We need to save money so we can travel abroad.; I'd rather invest in sustainable energy than fossil fuels.; I think we should try to do without a car and rely on public transport.; He said he can save some of his salary if he really tries.; You can't spend your money and invest it.

▶ **6.3** **1.** They brought up their children to protect the environment.; **2.** It's better to do without luxuries than run out of money.; **3.** I really can save money by cooking at home.; **4.** She's the only qualified accountant, so there are many issues she has to deal with.; **5.** You can't give all your money to charity and keep it for your children—you have to choose one option.

▶ **6.4** **1.** Are there many things that you've had to do without?; **2.** Do you have an emergency fund put aside in case you lose your job?; **3.** Do you go through your bills every month?

▶ **6.5**

A: This jacket fits perfectly. How does it look?

B: It looks great. I think you should buy it . . . What are you doing with your smartphone?

A: I'm just checking an app.

B: Huh? Why?

A: Well, I want to know more about this jacket and the company that made it—like how the workers are treated, whether the company protects the environment, you know. You can't get that from the label.

B: And you can find out all that using this app? How does it work?

A: It's really simple. You just look up a product and read the comments to find out more.

B: Really? Where do these comments come from?

A: From people all over the world. Anyone can upload comments on any product. You can click recommend or avoid, and give reasons. Then the information is all shared, and each product gets a rating.

B: Is it reliable? I mean, people can lie.

A: Maybe . . . but at least I'll have a general idea about the product. I want to make sure my money goes to help others and not to profit some company that treats their employees badly. And anyway, it only takes a second. You should try it—you can scan any barcode and check out the product. There are millions of products you can check out now.

B: Seems interesting. I think I'll give it a try. So are you going to get that jacket or not?

A: Yes, I am! Luckily, the ratings are good!

Unit 7

▶ **7.1**

A: You know, studies show that in a decade or two, people will be able to live much longer than now. Won't that be cool?

B: How much longer?

A: Well, the longest a human can live at the moment is about 120 years, but with medical innovations and new drugs, they think it may be possible to extend that four or five times eventually.

B: You're kidding! That would mean living five or six hundred years. That's crazy!

A: Apparently not. Scientists have found a way to extend the lifespan of mice by 50 percent already. And they're beginning to design new drugs to increase that even more. If it works on mice, it could eventually work on humans, right?

B: That's stretching it. Mice and humans are so different from each other!

A: Well, some experts believe that the first person to live 500 years might be alive already. Wouldn't you like that? Just imagine having all that time to do so many different things. It would be like seeing into the future.

B: Hmm. Just imagine working in the office for 500 years! And anyway, how would the Earth cope with all the people?

A: Well, I doubt that everyone could afford the treatment. It'll just be rich people, at least at first.

B: So normal people will die at 80 or 90, but the rich will live to 500? I don't like the sound of that.

A: Yeah, but it'll probably become more affordable, so everyone benefits in the end. I'd sure like to live a long, long life. You could have multiple careers.

B: Well, the most important thing is we should be healthy. No one would want to live hundreds of years sick in bed.

A: No, that's true. Health is key, and I believe it's important to have a better quality of life than just quantity.

▶ **7.2 1.** In the future, scientists believe that humans will be able to live hundreds of years.; **2.** With medical innovations and new drugs, I think all cancers will soon be curable.; **3.** We need a breakthrough in antibiotic research soon. Some bacteria are already resistant to all current antibiotics.

▶ **7.3** People might live to 150 in the future.; Doctors should be able to cure most serious diseases within a few decades.; With remote treatment, we won't need to visit the hospital or clinic so often.

▶ **7.4 1.** Robots might take over from doctors eventually.; **2.** Surgeons won't be replaced by machines for a long time.; **3.** New technology has led to many medical innovations.; **4.** Scientists are developing robots that look like human beings.; **5.** Medical scientists should be able to learn a lot from the space program.

▶ **7.5 1.** That cookie was meant for your brother!; **2.** The company organized a blood donation drive.; **3.** My grandfather suffered from Alzheimer's disease.; **4.** I bought these really cool shoes for a bargain!; **5.** Mama Rosa's bakery is the best place to buy fresh bread.; **6.** Scientists have found a way to extend the lifespan of mice.; **7.** San Francisco's Golden Gate is a popular tourist attraction.; **8.** The manager called a meeting to discuss the team's next project.; **9.** Mixed marriages are becoming more common these days.; **10.** The huge bear charged towards him.

▶ **7.6** Modern prosthetics are amazing—a high-tech combination of cutting edge software and materials, carefully made to suit each individual. They can be made to perform sophisticated movements, and some can now even be controlled by thought. But until recently, one important thing was missing: the sense of feeling.

Lacking feeling means that unless an amputee is looking, it's impossible to know what they are holding, and it's all too easy to grip something too tightly and break it. But recent developments in prosthetics technology promise to change this. Scientists have successfully wired sensors placed on artificial fingers to sensory nerves in an amputee's body. The result is that the amputee is able to feel pressure and even texture when using the prosthetic hand. This goes a long way to making people feel the prosthetic is part of them.

In addition, amputees can use sensory feedback to adjust their movements. This gives them a lot more control, even allowing them to perform delicate movements—like twisting the stem of a cherry. And for the first time, they don't need to look at their hand to see if they are gripping too tightly or not tightly enough.

What are the next steps for prosthetic technology? Scientists are looking forward to the day in-the-not-too-distant-future when the whole system can be implanted under the skin. Soon, we may be looking at smaller, wireless prosthetics that can provide sensory feedback and be controlled using the mind.

Unit 8

▶ **8.1** In many ways, life is a series of milestones—leaving our parents, getting our first job, passing a driving test, getting married, having children, and retiring, to name just a few. However, these milestones have changed a lot over the years and also differ widely from country to country. For example, attitudes towards marriage and the age at which people marry have changed significantly over the years.

People all over the world now marry at a later age—or not at all—although the actual age depends on the country. Overall, people in richer countries tend to marry later than those in developing countries. Germany has the oldest average age of marriage, at over 33, while at the other end of the scale are several countries in Africa, such as Niger and Chad, where it is common to be married by the age of 20. Women everywhere marry earlier than men, although this trend has been changing slowly over the last few decades. As societal pressure to marry continues to decrease, especially in Western countries, more people often choose to remain single. In 1960, over seven in ten people in the United States were married, but today, less than half are.

Another milestone that has changed in many countries is the decision of when to have kids, or even whether to have children at all. This also reflects changing

attitudes. In countries such as South Korea, Japan, and Australia, the average age for women having their first child is now over 30. In contrast, in Angola and Bangladesh, women give birth for the first time at an average age of around 18. These days, many women are choosing never to have children.

While cultural attitudes continue to change and are reflected in changing milestones, it is worth noting that marriage is still common. In most countries, 80 percent of men and women are married by the age of 50.

▶ **8.2** She'll have moved house by October.; They'll have been living in San Francisco for six months soon.; I won't have left town by then.; He won't have finished work by that time.

▶ **8.3** **1.** She'll have finished university in three years.; **2.** You won't have passed your driving test by the end of the year.; **3.** He won't have finished his homework by then.; **4.** You'll have arrived in Hawaii by this time next week.; **5.** I'll have started my new job when you next see me.

▶ **8.4** **1.** In May, I'll have lived here for exactly 10 years.; **2.** Don't call at six. I won't have finished work.; **3.** I'll have graduated by this time next year.; **4.** When I've finished this one, I'll have written five novels.

▶ **8.5**

A: Are you happier now than when you were in high school?

B: Happier? Definitely. High school was OK, but I love college. And it's great to have my own place and be independent . . . Why do you ask?

A: Oh, I was just reading about life milestones. It got me thinking.

B: Really? How about you, then? Are you more satisfied with your life now that you're in college?

A: Yes, I am. High school was hard for me. Life now is more fun for sure. But I'm not sure about the future.

B: What do you mean?

A: I'll need to get a serious job soon, but I don't know what I want to do. And good jobs are hard to come by . . . Aren't you worried?

B: No, not really. I'm not interested in a career—at least not now. I want to travel and see the world after I graduate. Work overseas. Do some volunteering. Maybe I'll think about my career when I'm 30.

A: 30? That's way too late for me. I hope I'll have found a good career before then.

B: Hmm. I don't think I'll ever settle down. There's just too much to do and see, people to meet, you know . . .

A: You don't want a family? Kids?

B: I can't imagine having kids. I guess I might change my mind in the future, though. Anyway, there's plenty of time, right?

A: I'm not so sure about that. Time seems to fly by. Before you know it, we'll be old and retired.

B: Yeah. Mind you, I heard that people are happiest when they're old. So maybe that's not a problem!

Unit 9

▶ **9.1** It's the stuff of sci-fi movies: robots have taken over the world, and humans are fighting back. Of course, this could never happen—or could it?

Microsoft co-founder Bill Gates has said that while robots won't be as intelligent as humans for several more decades, we should be concerned about super intelligent robots in the future. Gates is joined by Elon Musk, founder of Tesla Motors and SpaceX, who believes that these robots could present the greatest threat to the survival of humans ever.

Scientist Stephen Hawking agrees with Gates and Musk. Explaining why, Hawking says that humans, limited by slow biological evolution, couldn't compete with robots, which have the potential to learn and evolve faster and faster. These super robots could learn to assemble themselves and eventually gain control over humans.

However, it's not all bad news. These experts point out that if we can create strong procedures to monitor and control robots, we can avoid this scary outcome. They add that robots have enormous potential benefits for society—helping rescue people in times of disaster, performing surgery, and doing dangerous jobs, to name just a few. Robots could even help get rid of disease and poverty. But, they warn, we need to act now, before it is too late.

▶ **9.2** **1.** If you bought a fitness tracker, what would you use it for?; **2.** If you get home late tonight, what will you do?; **3.** If she won the lottery, how would she spend her prize money?; **4.** If you were me, would you take that job?

▶ **9.3** What's your favorite smartphone app?; I saw a really interesting movie about robots.; If AI gained control over humans, life would be miserable.; Rapid innovation in technology leads to very different lifestyles.

▶ **9.4** **1.** Soon, everybody will have a smartphone.; **2.** My fitness tracker records my average heartrate.; **3.** This app monitors the temperature of my living room.; **4.** He bought a camera with his first paycheck.; **5.** There are several good cafés in the neighborhood.

▶ **9.5** **1.** She learned to operate the device quickly.; **2.** Robots will learn to perform complex surgery.; **3.** There'll be more robots in the military in coming years.; **4.** The professor did not elaborate further what had gone wrong with the research.; **5.** You'll need to separate this batch so your product doesn't get contaminated.

▶ **9.6** The world has been through three major industrial revolutions in the last few hundred years. Each time, thousands of people lost their jobs as new technology completely changed how they worked. But each time, people adapted and the new technology gave rise to new fields of industry and new jobs.

Now we are entering the fourth industrial revolution, and many people are rightly concerned about the massive changes that are predicted. Some experts believe that this time is different and will result in huge numbers of people losing their jobs permanently. However, optimists believe that, as before, we will adapt and find work in new areas. It's happened before and it could happen again.

Experts predict that 65 percent of children now entering primary school will end up working in jobs that don't yet exist. While it is true that automation and robots will replace humans in large numbers, it is also true that a lot of these robots will be designed to work alongside humans, and this will create a whole range of new jobs.

There will be a need to educate and train people so they are equipped with the skills needed to work with the technology. And as long as existing workers are re-trained, they can adapt to the new work environment. It will be challenging, a time of great change and massive job losses, but humanity will adapt and move on.

Unit 10

▶ **10.1**

A: Hey. How was your chat with Mike? Did you tell him about the problem at work?

B: Yeah, I did, but it wasn't much help.

A: Seriously? He didn't give you any good advice?

B: No. In fact, I don't think he was even listening to me. He seemed distracted and I had to keep repeating everything!

A: That's very odd . . . He's usually a good listener. I had a chat with him just the other day about changing jobs. He seemed pretty focused and listened thoughtfully to my ideas.

B: Hmm. Well, this time I don't think he was paying attention at all. And he kept getting messages on his phone.

A: Really? Sounds like something was going on.

B: Yeah, I think so. In the end, I asked him if it was a bad time to talk.

A: Oh yeah, and what did he say?

B: He didn't hear me! He was busy with his messages. So I gave up trying to explain.

A: Oh no! . . . I'm sorry it ended that way. So what's your next plan?

B: I'm going to try talking to Nikki. She knows the general situation and she's a good friend.

A: Mm. Good idea. Nikki's a good listener. She may even be able to recommend someone who can help out.

B: Yeah, I hope so . . . here's what I wanted to tell her . . . (*gets cut off by A getting message on his phone*)

A: Oh, hang on, sorry, I need to reply to this.

B: Oh no, not you too!

▶ **10.2** **1.** "Could you focus on her lecture, Chris?"; **2.** "I'll definitely finish the report today."; **3.** "His speech was really long."; **4.** "Kyle, present your paper to the class."

▶ **10.3** I want every student to listen in silence.; She listened to my complaint, but not sympathetically.; But you promised you would help me!

▶ **10.4** **1.** That was a terrible movie.; **2.** I really enjoyed that lecture.; **3.** Don't you think that was a difficult test?; **4.** I highly recommend you hire him. He's a very good worker.; **5.** She's a rude child!

▶ **10.5** **1.** Did Irene give a presentation on hearing aids?; **2.** I can't believe Tim said that to the waiter!; **3.** Why is Teddy apologizing to Peter?; **4.** Is Pablo the person in charge of invoices?

▶ **10.6** In today's world, it is often difficult to listen to other people. We're all busy and we're constantly distracted by message alerts and notifications on our smartphones. But it's not only outside distractions that affect us. The way we talk also has a powerful effect on how people listen to us.

There are certain habits that many people have that make it harder for others to listen to them. In his TED Talk, *How to speak so that people want to listen*, Julian Treasure identifies several bad habits that we should try to avoid.

The first is gossip—speaking ill of someone who's not there. It's not a nice habit and you know there's a high chance the person gossiping *to* you will probably gossip *about* you as well.

Then there is the habit of being negative. Nobody wants to listen to someone who's pessimistic about everything. And a person who's negative is also usually a person who complains. Everybody tends to complain at one time or another, but a person who constantly does so becomes irritating and hard to focus on.

And finally there is exaggeration. We all like to embellish the truth every now and then, but when it becomes a habit, it's hard to know when the person is lying or not. And once people find it hard to trust your word, they find it hard to listen to you.

These are just some of the bad habits we can fall into when we speak. If we can avoid them, we will be become more powerful speakers, and that in turn will lead to people paying more attention to us when we speak.

Unit 11

▶ **11.1**

A: Hi everybody and welcome to our camp. You're going to have a great weekend—we have a range of activities that will help you disconnect from your devices and reconnect with each other and with nature. You'll find all the details in your welcome packs, but some of our highlights are: guided mountain hikes, yoga, meditation, and our workshops on nature, art, and creative writing. Okay, before we get started, I'll run through a few house rules. Firstly, talking about work is taboo here. Okay? And that includes any kind of networking. Next, no digital tech. No laptops, no tablets, and no Internet.

B: Phones are okay, right? Like for taking photos?

A: No, phones are out too. No devices at all. This is about becoming mindful of where you are— phones and other devices are just a distraction.

B: Uh, okay.

A: Just a couple more things—no clocks or watches are allowed. You won't need them. And lastly, this is a tobacco- and alcohol-free place.

C: How about the food?

A: All the food is fresh, locally grown, and organic. And it's cruelty-free. No meat or animal products. It's healthy and delicious—you'll love it . . . Okay, so what will you get out of your time here? Apart from having a lot of fun, enjoying nature, and making friends, you'll slow down, you'll de-stress, and you'll become more mindful and aware. And you'll sleep better and deeper. That will help you restore your energy as well as become more creative. Sound good? Okay. Let's get started.

▶ **11.2** Noise and lots of distractions take a toll on the brain.; An increasing number of people are looking for a slower pace of life.; The email that I wrote today was a long and complicated one.; I often work in the evening if I have an urgent deadline.

▶ **11.3** **1.** There was a hair on the floor.; **2.** I heard noise coming from downstairs.; **3.** There was glass on the kitchen table.; **4.** How's the business?; **5.** Is there a room for me?

▶ **11.4** **1.** I'm taking a trip to the countryside this weekend.; **2.** I need to get away from the city for a few days.; **3.** Spending time at the beach helps me relax.; **4.** It'll be good to take things easy for a while.; **5.** I've booked a room in a quiet hotel.

▶ **11.5** The growth of the Slow City movement, or Cittaslow, spelled C-I-T-T-A-S-L-O-W, is a response to increased globalization, a world in which cities are becoming more and more similar. Cittaslow's goal is to encourage cities around the world to support their local traditions, retain their uniqueness, and preserve nature.

One such example is Hanok Village, about 240 kilometers south of Seoul. Hanok Village, located in the city of Jeonju, was certified as a Slow City in 2010, and features over 800 old-style houses; it is full of historical charm. Visitors can enjoy traditional Korean life and food, sitting on heated floors.

In 2016, the whole city of Jeonju was certified as a slow city. This was in recognition of its efforts to preserve its traditions and natural environment. There are clear benefits to becoming a slow city for locals and visitors alike. Since 2010, there has been a large increase in the number of tourists visiting Jeonju, going from 3.5 million to nearly 10 million in 2015. Jeonju is one of a growing number of slow cities in Asia.

Although most slow cities are situated in Europe, several, like Jeonju, are now in Asia. The trend for people to want to slow down in a slow city is sure to continue in Asia and the rest of the world. And that is something to savor, slowly.

Unit 12

▶ **12.1**

A: How was the meeting with the potential new business partner? You went with Lewis, right?

B: Yeah. It went well. We'll probably sign a contract with them soon. But there's a small problem.

A: Oh yeah? What's that?

B: I think they tried to bribe Lewis. When we left, I saw them hand him an envelope.

A: An envelope? What was in it?

B: Some cash. I found out later. Lewis said they insisted he take it. They said it was just a small token of appreciation for his efforts.

A: You're kidding! He shouldn't have accepted it! I think you need to report this to the boss!

B: No, no. I think Lewis needs to resolve the situation. I'll try to persuade him to explain that it was a misunderstanding and hand the money to the company. He needs to know it will affect me too!

A: Yeah, that sounds sensible. But what if you can't persuade him? What will you do?

B: That's a tough question. I don't want to go behind his back, but I think I'll have to do something. It wouldn't be right to keep quiet . . . What would you do?

A: Hmm . . . Well, if it had been me, I'd probably sit down with him over a coffee. I'd be honest, and explain the difficult situation he'd put us both in. I'd let him know what I thought.

B: Mm, that might work. Yeah . . . I think I'll do that.

A: Well, good luck. Let's hope it works out okay for everyone.

B: Yeah. Thanks. Hey, keep this to yourself, of course.

A: Yes, of course. Talk later.

▶ **12.2** I would have told you if I'd known how you felt.; I would have won if you hadn't cheated.; I wouldn't have complained if you hadn't mentioned it.; I wouldn't have passed the exam if I hadn't studied so hard.

▶ **12.3** **1.** I wouldn't have finished on time . . .; **2.** I would have resigned . . .; **3.** He wouldn't have known about it . . .; **4.** He wouldn't have been angry . . .; **5.** She would have got the job . . .

▶ **12.4** **1.** They wouldn't have gotten married if they didn't love each other.; **2.** It would have been quicker if we'd taken a taxi.; **3.** She would have come to the party if you'd invited her.; **4.** If it hadn't been so expensive, I would have bought it.; **5.** If I'd known about it, I would have said something.

▶ **12.5** Wildlife trade is a serious and deadly business. It promotes corruption and some of the money made helps fund armed conflict.

Aiming to reduce the scale of this destructive trade is WildLeaks, a website designed to encourage wildlife crime whistleblowers. It got off to a good start. In its first three months, there were as many as 24 serious tip-offs, way beyond the creators' expectations. These tip-offs were diverse: illegal logging and fishing, poaching of elephants, tigers, lions and leopards, chimpanzee trafficking, and importing of illegal wildlife from Africa into the United States. All information relating to these crimes can be viewed on WildLeaks's website. However, information about those who have reported these crimes is kept confidential.

One example of how these tip-offs make a difference: There was a tip-off about elephant poaching. It resulted in the naming of several high-level people involved in the 2012 slaughter of over 20,000 elephants for their ivory tusks. This is a huge number when you consider that the number of elephants in Africa today is only 400,000, down from nearly 30 million 200 years ago.

WildLeaks won't stop wildlife trade on its own. But it is beginning to make a difference, and is a small part of the solution to stopping this terrible trade. Every case of wildlife trade that is brought to light by the website is crucial in the battle to keep these species from becoming extinct.

Credits